SHREVEPORT
LIBRARY

Presented by

Allis Family

Wild-water Canoeing and Kayaking

A **Jolex** SPORT PUBLICATION

Wild-water Canoeing and Kayaking

Steidle

Photo Credits:

Robert Steidle, Ulla Steidle,
Alto Nuernberger

Drawings: Anina Westphalen

ISBN: 0-89149-026-4 paper

Published by:
JOLEX INC.,
Paramus, New Jersey

Distributed by:
THE JOHN OLSON COMPANY
299 Forest ave., Box 767
Paramus, New Jersey 07652

Translated from German by:
Gertrud Menzel-Collin

Adapted for North America
by Charles Farmer

Copyright © by BLV Verlagsgesellschaft mbH,
Munich 1976
Title of the original german edition:
,,Wildwasserfahren"

About the author

Robert W. Steidle has devoted the past 16 years to the art of wild-water canoeing and kayaking. In 1964, he contributed to the science of the sport by improving the design of wild-water boats.

"Wild-water Canoeing and Kayaking" was written for the beginner but contains so much wild-water lore that it is invaluable to anyone who challenges wild-water. The author is highly regarded in Europe and, most specifically, in Germany where he has long conducted wild-water schools.

Today, Bob Steidle is a professor of art, but claims his heart pumps to the tune of churning, roaring angry river currents.

Table of Contents

The art of kayaking and canoeing

After beaching our boats, we lay on the sand and rested. We had returned to civilization after a hard cruise from Dollart to Cuxhaven, across the shallows, traversing the North Sea to Sylt. We felt quietly satisfied and pleased with ourselves. A sunbather came up to us and warned that the boats were much to small. "And besides," he added, "why use a boat without a motor?"

Other self-proclaimed experts hold the same view. South Sea Islanders, for instance, and Eskimos from Alaska to Baffin Land use motors on their large umiaks. They are no longer familiar with kayaking and Eskimo rolling.

But despite modern man's infatuation with motor-driven vehicles, kayaking and canoeing are booming. The motorless movement began 90 years ago when Sir Baden-Powell, who founded the British Boy Scouts, paddled the waters of Great Britain in a 'small portable canvas boat.' In the 1920's, new life was injected with the invention of the foldboat. Today, the arrival of ABS plastic increases the popularity of canoeing and kayaking by decreasing the cost of purchasing a boat.

Our slender crafts are not only at home on every water, they are also small enough to take anywhere. A canoe or kayak enables us to meet nature herself. Far away from the noisy trumpets of nothingness, boat and tent seem somewhat anachronistic. In these days, we paddlers, too, must swim the great tourist stream in order to discover our paradises. It is possible but it takes effort.

Robert Steidle, skier, climber and sworn to the lure of wild-water has found isolated paradises. This was revealed in his first book *Alpenflusse-Kajakflusse*.

This is a new book by Steidle. Would our 'hard' sport not give so much pleasure, I would call this book a 'systematic' introduction and instruction to wild-water paddling. Nevertheless, this book is based on the experience of nature which is as indispensable with kayaking and canoeing as with climbing. Steidle starts from his broad knowledge but concentrates on wild-water canoeing

and kayaking. This is by no means a criticism of leisurely touring! The wild-water paddler is literally at home on all waters. And even the most relaxed touring requires a range of experience. The good paddle stroke is always preceded by the knowledge of how to execute it. This book is a reliable source for learning how to paddle wild-water. It is a handbook that informs in detail how to perform strokes as well as when to use them. Besides the basics, Steidle includes topics of interest to the 'old pros.' This book is indispensable as well as entertaining. Consider Steidle's advice to practice the Eskimo roll on a meadow. What an idea! *Herbert Rittlinger*

Introduction

Wild-water sports are increasing in popularity. With more canoeists and kayakers, there is a greater demand for reliable tips about equipment and more detailed instruction concerning wild-water techniques.

Like Alpine skiing, Alpine kayaking is attracting more people. Individuals want to participate and not merely observe. Hardship, danger, discomfort inspire rather than discourage a certain few.

Therefore, this book will help increase the pleasure of wild-water cruising by improving the skill of the canoeist or kayaker. In the long run, a better boater is a safer one as well.

Safety in wild-water cruising depends on three factors: technique, equipment, and tactics. These topics are the central issues of the book. Equipment and tactics are mainly matters of personal knowledge, judgment, and experience. As an example, the difficulty rating of a wild river may not accurately reflect how well an individual can handle it. This justifies the advice to tackle a wild-water stretch that is one class too easy rather than one class too difficult. Techniques, however, develop from knowledge, physical ability, and practice. Practicing is a process of learning that takes less and less time with increasing independence from the instructor. Practice should occur periodically under expert supervision where progress is noted and mistakes corrected. The first step in learning a technique is mental training.

The correct technique, both in its basic and advanced form, is described in detail. Pictures, graphs, films, and demonstrations can give the trainee an idea of the individual steps of a movement. When the technique is perfected, the result occurs with a minimum of energy expended.

The aim of the training is not only to learn a perfect technique but to improve the paddler's awareness and splitsecond decision-making as well. He should be motivated to experiment continually with boat, paddle and current. Only by executing the techniques when he is not required to do so can he hope to avoid using them as lifesaving formulas. Each boat, each paddle, each river requires slightly different techniques. The boatman has to decide how this can be done while floating the river. The self-reliance gained from successfully negotiating wild-water cannot be transmitted by any trainer or book. How automatic should a technique be? Does a completely automatic execution give more safety than the ability to react instantaneously to new situations by a number of alternatives? The Eskimo roll, for instance, is effective for righting the kayak after capsizing. However, it can be deadly in shallow water or in front of a rocky wall.

Wild-water paddling is strenuous and conditions the body for stamina and endurance. No other physical exercise prepares the muscles for paddling besides paddling itself.

In this book, all the techniques known today and applied in wild-water are described in a progressive order from easy to difficult. A technique can be learned by practicing 6 hours a day for about 5 days. The term *technique* as used in this book covers all paddle strokes and the resultant motion of the boat. A technique is learned best on smooth water. A *maneuver* results from the application of one or several differing techniques in defined currents as observed in wild-water. Ferry gliding, for example, results from backpaddling at a defined angle to the current. Maneuvers are preferably learned in haystacks and roller waves.

Tactics result from one or several maneuvers combined to reach or keep a desired course. Tactics are learned primarily by running wild rivers.

Coordination of the three factors, paddle, boat and current is rather complicated for the beginner. The training of the wild-water technique is discussed in the chapters, "Training on Lakes," "Practicing in Haystacks," "Training in a Roller Wave," and "Training in Wild-Water." A "wild" or undisciplined paddling style is wasteful because it ends up in low efficiency despite much energy consumption. To correct this style, the boatman should practice with someone who can point out mistakes and offer helpful pointers. But even solitary practice sessions can improve paddling techniques. Begin in smooth water and gradually advance to haystacks, roller waves, and easy wild-water. The slalom with time limits and penalty points is the ultimate in disciplined paddling, requiring repeated practice periods. Experience can be accumulated through learning one's faults and weaknesses on smooth water. Correcting them before floating wild-water increases the fun, exhilaration, and safety of canoeing and kayaking.

Equipment

Designs and Characteristics of Wild-Water Boats

The "ideal boat" is heatedly debated among wild-water paddlers. Even though an ideal boat does not exist, there are designs that are better suited for wild-water cruising. Because a kayak or canoe is an extension of the boater, he feels strongly about the way it responds and how it reacts in heavy wild-water. He commonly solves problems through his own ingenuity, which in turn gives fresh input to the design of wild-water craft.

Wild-water boats are difficult to design primarily because there is neither rudder nor stern board. Steering is achieved merely by trim and paddle. A wild-water boat should have maximum forward speed and should neither sheer nor broach. It should permit easy lateral displacement and have good pivoting and turning ability in both the righted and bracing position. In addition, the craft should be equally maneuverable backpaddling as well as forward stroking. Moreover, it should slide over rocks, logs, and dams and should be usable after prolonged upturned gliding across multiple obstructions.

The boat should withstand wild-water breaking over the bow and be responsive in heavy current. For a kayak, the Eskimo roll should be easily executed in sucking currents without detrimental effects on the craft. The paddler should have good visual contact with potential obstacles downstream when seated in a canoe or kayak.

Depending on weight, weight distribution, and volume, the different design characteristics have differing effects on the behavior of a craft in wild-water. The ideal combination of these characteristics can only be achieved by approximation. It varies from river to river and from paddler to paddler. The following compilation is an objective evaluation. The wild-water enthusiast can choose his own "ideal" combination.

"Rocker" (Pronounced Curve to the Boat's Keel)

The pronounced curve to the keel is preferred when maneuverability is most important. That is, for slalom boats and wild-water touring craft.

Advantages: Boats with a pronounced rocker in their keel are highly maneuverable. They are easy to handle in ferry gliding and easy to swing. The pivot point shifts backward at high speed, thus holding a steering line more easily.

Disadvantages: Unfortunately, the maneuverable boat tends to sheer. Even slight turbulence deviates the craft from its straight forward course and the stern broaches. This becomes particularly evident in narrow bends. At high speed, the boat rises markedly and resistance increases, making movement across heavy current difficult.

Straight Keel

The straight keel promotes maximum speed and superiority in holding a true steering line. That is, for wild-water racing and downriver racing boats and for foldboats and canoes for smooth water and lakes.

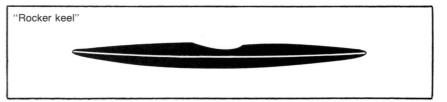

"Rocker keel"

Advantages: The high speed of straight keel boats is mainly a consequence of their hardly rising bow. The higher directional stability in haystacks and cross-winds may facilitate cruising in big water. In addition, such a craft draws less water.

Disadvantages: A straight keel craft is less maneuverable at normal trim. It goes with the current. As a consequence, mistakes made in boulder-studded wild-water are difficult to remedy.

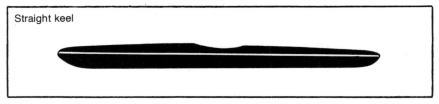

Straight keel

Rounded Gunwales

The new synthetics permit designs which better meet the requirements of white-water sports than do the traditional foldboats.

Advantages: Boats with rounded gunwales are largely insensitive to plunging waves, whether they break over the side or pound down on the deck. They are easy to roll in wild-water and react good-naturedly to paddling mistakes. And there are no sharp edges to injure the boater.

Disadvantages: The rounded gunwale causes loss of speed in rapids, dams, and rollers.

Sharp-Edged Deck

The sharp-edged deck is the traditional design of the foldboat. It has a cross-section with a sharp distinction between bottom and deck. It is used today for downriver racing.

Advantages: Because the edged deck does not detract from the speed of the craft at the bottom of rapids and in running dams, the boat escapes easier from the dangerous back eddy. Particularly fast in rollers, the boat can be speeded up ("plum-stone effect") with the right volume distribution and a not too flat deck. The lateral edges easily shed water, especially in mild wild-water. Of special interest to the slalom paddler, the

edged deck craft is swift in the bracing position when crossing currents. And maneuverability does not suffer in heavy water where waves break over the boat.

Disadvantages: The edges are sensitive to water from above and the side, particularly if the craft has a low bottom and a steep deck. And there is always the possibility of injury occurring on the sharp edges. Such boats (except the narrow racing boats) are hard to roll in wild-water and difficult to brace. If the bottom is low, they tend to broach. On passing very steep dams, they may even be pushed backward, resulting in negative consequences.

Rounded gunwales

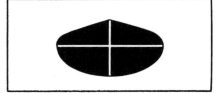

Sharp-edged deck

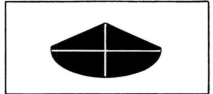

Main Rib: Elliptical or Circular

The dispute over whether a craft should have a flat or rounded main rib is as old as shipbuilding itself. As a matter of fact, the Vikings decided in favor of the markedly rounded main rib when they built their warships, which were among the best ever made. In recent times, many high quality canoes and kayaks have been made with a rounded main rib.

Advantages: Boats with a rounded main rib show balance in turbulent waters and high stability when bracing. They do not tip over suddenly and are responsive to foot, hip, and paddle bracing. As a result, they are easy to Eskimo roll and suited for the draw technique. The boats are superior at holding a true steering line in high waves and are affected little by waves breaking over the sides. In connection with transport and storage, such a boat has better flexible strength.

Circular main rib

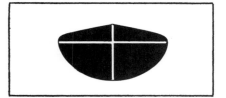

Disadvantages: Naturally, such a boat demands a highly developed sense of balance from the start. It draws more water and, accordingly, its carrying capacity is less than that of a boat with a flat bottom.

Main Rib: Flat

The flat main rib has the shape of a flattened U and is used frequently in boat construction.

Advantages: The flat bottom boat's stability is attractive to the beginner. With gear aboard, the insignificant draft is a positive quality. Its great carrying capacity is a plus for heavy slalom combatants.

Disadvantages: Even though the flat bottom boat is safe in smooth water, it tends to tip over suddenly in heavy water. Once at the point of tipping, it can hardly be righted again. Such boats are sensitive to side water and due to high friction, are not very fast.

Flat main rib

Chances are good that the flat bottom boat will be damaged in transport or storage.

Boats with Considerable Rise at Bow and Stern

The original designs of the Eskimo kayak, dugout canoe Viking ship, and fishing boat incorporate a rise at both bow and stern for practical purposes. This design was always used for the Eskimo kayak, whether built as a foldboat or a rigid plastic boat, and the canoe. More recently, wild-water touring boats followed the tradition. In fact, if slalom competition did not include several impractical rules, nobody would have thought of bringing bow and stern of wild-water boats down to water level.

Advantages: The boat with the rise at bow and stern can cross obstacles easily and will resist getting hung up under a boulder or downed timber. At the same time, ferry gliding, crossing, and upstream cruising are easier because bow or stern do not as inevitably pierce the next wave. Due to dry riding, such boats are fast on big water and have only a slight loss of speed when passing dams, rapids, and rollers because they submerge to a lesser degree.

Disadvantages: The boat dashes from wave to wave in a nervous run. As a matter of course, such boats are less suited for slalom competition because slicing the gates is more difficult. The higher speed is thus counterbalanced by the risk of penalty points when fouling the poles.

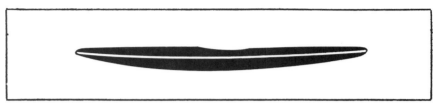

Bow and stern both rise

Boat with Markedly Rounded Bow and Stern

The "Swiss banana" was designed by Swiss wild-water experts to run extremely intricate rapids and has completely rounded bow and stern. Since then, less specialized types of craft too show more rounding of bow and stern.

Advantages: Most important is the reduced danger of being caught in obstructions. Likewise the rounded bow and stern makes injury during training less of a possibility. In addition, the rounded design provides greater buoyancy in bow and stern.

Disadvantages: Actually, the moderately rounded design has no disadvantages except in downriver races. The severely rounded boat, however, offers higher resistance in roller waves and causes considerable loss in speed when plunging into steep rapids and dams.

Flat Deck

The idea to build a covered kayak probably originated with the Eskimos. This made cruising possible where it was unimaginable before. They could then negotiate wild-water rivers and the ocean surf. The covered design prevents swamping as well as affecting the nautical qualities of the lightweight boats.

Kayak training in a roller wave is impossible in an open craft.

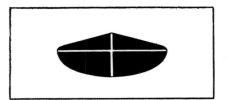

Flat deck

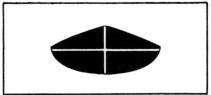

Steep deck

Advantages: The flat deck produces a calmer ride. It is easy to roll and insensitive to side water. After an upset, the craft takes on less water.

Disadvantages: Because the flat deck boat is actually part of the river when afloat, the boater rides wet. In addition, it has an inherent instability against water pressure that is encountered, for example, in big rollers.

Steep Deck

Advantages: The steep deck floats on top of the water instead of in the current. This enables the paddler to ride dry. It also possesses a higher inherent stability against water pressure, making it unnecessary to reinforce the deck.

Disadvantages: Major problems may result from the fact that the boat may emerge too steeply in rollers and be caught by an obstacle. This is especially true with lightweight craft.

Length of Boat

The trend is toward shorter boats. Even though some wild-water experts have experimented with craft of 12 to 13 feet (3.8 m), most agree that 13 feet (4 m) or longer is ideal. For the intermediate, a handy, maneuverable boat within the 13 foot range is recommended. However, the novice may experience difficulties in straight ahead paddling. But in the long run, the shorter boat is better suited for persons with less physical strength.

One-man Boats of 13 feet (4.0 to 4.2 m):

Advantages: The short boat has less water resistance and is highly maneuverable. In heavy water with many obstacles, the craft is very fast. Because the short boat is responsive, the paddler learns the correct technique rapidly.

Disadvantages: What is maneuverable in the hands of an expert, is

goosey under the direction of a beginner or intermediate. The short boat drops more steeply in rapids and behind dams as well as emerges more steeply from roller waves. As a result, the boat can be on the brink of capsizing or being swamped often with only the expertise of the boater keeping the craft upright.

One-man Boats of 14 feet (4.2 to 4.5 m):

Long boats of 15 feet are mainly used in downriver races. Others are built as Eskimo kayaks with raised bow and stern.

Advantages: The long boat holds a true steering line in haystacks and on big water. It has an unequaled, balanced ride in rollers and souse holes, rapids and behind dams. However, sufficient buoyancy in bow and stern is important.

Disadvantages: The long boat is less maneuverable. It is difficult to turn, particularly if straight keeled, and hard to handle on intricate wild-water.

Beam

Often beam is mistakenly assumed to be synonymous with safety. In wild-water, however, resistance to

Canoeing in the short,
maneuverable C 2 is gaining
popularity.

capsizing that is found with a wide boat is less important than seaworthiness resulting from responsiveness to paddling and foot and hip bracing.

Broad-Beamed One-man Boat:
2 to 2$^{1}/_{2}$ feet (.65 to .75 m)

Advantages: The broad-beamed boat has high stability and great carrying capacity at low draft.

Disadvantages: While being stable in calm water, the broad-beamed boat is prone to overturning in turbulent stretches, especially if the craft is also flat bottomed. In this case, bracing is useless and rolling is nearly impossible. Because the entire bottom rides the water, it offers high re-sistance and runs slowly. Turned broadside in haystacks, rollers, or surf, it will inevitably capsize.

Narrow-Beamed One-man Boat:
1$^{1}/_{2}$ to 2 feet (.50 to .65 m)

In competition, because of dimensional requirements, the 2-foot (.60 m) beam became common.

Advantages: Narrow boats are easy to roll and brace. Therefore, tipping can be prevented by paddle bracing

in connection with hip and knee bracing. Moreover, these craft ride easily and offer low resistance in big water. Finally, they induce the paddler to learn a correct technique.

Disadvantages: The narrower shape has greater draft, lower carrying capacity, and lower stability, which offers difficulties to the beginner only.

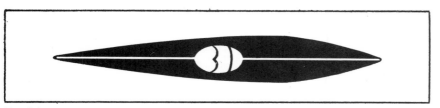

Swedeform

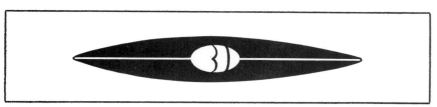

Symmetrical plan shape

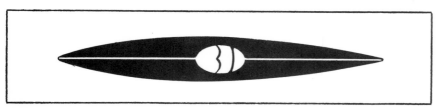

Fishform

Shapes

The shape of wild-water touring boats have hardly changed during the last few years. In general, the shapes that are easily maneuverable in forward and backward paddling are still used. In downriver racing, however, experience modified the shape of the boats, facilitating maximum speed as well as seaworthiness and maneuverability.

"Swedeform"

The shape of a craft has the point of widest beam slightly aft of the midpoint.

Advantages: Boats of this type with a rounded main rib are extremely fast and are found almost exclusively in wild-water downriver racing. They are easy to steer and to control in rollers. With the flat rib at the stern, ferry gliding is easy, making the craft well suited for back paddling in wild-water.

Disadvantages: Because the pivot point is before the center of gravity, this boat tends to sheer in haystacks, bends, and boulder studded wild-water. Moreover, it is sensitive to side wind and difficult to hold on line if it also has a pronounced rocker.

Symmetrical Shape

Advantages: Such a craft has good directional stability that provides easy turning and exact maneuvering in wild-water.

Disadvantages: The stern is not as responsive as that of the Swedeform boat.

Fishform

The fishform is wider toward the bow end of amidship. Such a craft is a touring rather than a wild-water boat.

Advantages: It exhibits high directional stability, even with a sharp V-rip in the bow section, and runs

smoothly. The V-rib adds greater speed.

Disadvantages: This type of boat is less maneuverable and tends to broach while ferry gliding. Due to the greater volume of the bow, the current can push the stern aside, which is dangerous where precise maneuvering is necessary. The low volume of the stern leads to unbalanced performance in roller waves.

The shape of a craft, its keel, and main rib should be seen in connection with the rib shape at bow and stern. In general, boats with sharp bow and rounded stern show properties similar to Swedeform boats.

Boat Building Materials

1. Foldboats

The foldboat established wild-water cruising as a sport. It withstood the test of crossing the Atlantic Ocean as well as most rivers on earth. Outstanding designers were primarily the Scotchman John McGregor and the Englishmen August Voigt and Curt Donat, who promoted their decisive ideas at the end of the last century. Later on, the architect Alfred Heurich developed today's foldboat design. J. Klepper was the first who launched it on the market.
Well-known foldboat pioneers were Carl J. Luther and Herbert Rittlinger, who cruised the Upper Amazon and Euphrates and led other Foldboat expeditions. In 1928, Franz Romer crossed the Atlantic as did Dr. Lindemann in 1956, both using a foldboat double seater.

Construction

Made of elastic woods, the skeletal elements consist of transverse ribs and longitudinal longerons. They are separable. This skeleton is covered by a hull of coated, watertight, rip-resistant fabric. The deck is made of

uncoated, waterproof fabric. They can be designed as single or double kayaks.

Advantages: The separated parts permit easy transportation and stowing. Because of an usually high bottom and good terminal stability, the foldboat possesses good nautical qualities on big wild-water, sometimes superior to those of fiberglass kayaks. The reliable directional stability and the already-mentioned good trim are seldom found with fiberglass wild-water kayaks.

Disadvantages: Due to its sharp edged shape and the less smooth surface, the foldboat is less maneuverable and more difficult to move laterally. High susceptibility to cuts and other damage to the hull requires immediate repair and interrupts the trip. Under severe water pressure – for example, if you broadside into an obstacle – the craft can become a mousetrap by breaking in two. The edged design makes it sensitive to water pouring onto the deck, which is partly counterbalanced by the high shape. Higher weight and friction are responsible for less acceleration and a slower run.

2. Fiberglass Boats

No one knows who was the first to

use fiberglass in kayak and canoe building. However, the author remembers a student making kayaks of fiberglass impregnated with resin in the late '50's, just outside of Munich. Probably, several inventors had the idea simultaneously. And sportsmen, always ready to experiment, may have built suitable kayaks long before the manufacturers. In the early '60's, the fiberglass craft replaced the foldboat in the wild-water field and became the pacemaker.

Construction

The hull and seat, with the cockpit rim, are made of fiberglass impregnated with polyester resin. The hull consists of two shells cemented together. They are made in so-called negative molds by hand feeding or jet molding. Durability can be increased by adding diolene fabric. Highest strength is reached by combining fiberglass, diolene fabric, and epoxy resin and carbon fibers.

Fiberglass boats are built as single or double kayaks, single or double sport canoes, or as open touring canoes in varying designs. Fiberglass is preferred for competition.

Advantages: Design and nautical qualities of the fiberglass boat set the pace for all other craft. At present, the optimum combination of boat shape

to the hydrodynamics of wild-water can be achieved only with synthetics. Due to the smooth surface, the boat easily slides across obstacles, has low frictional resistance in water, and slows only slightly in rollers and wild-water. The paddler has excellent control over the boat with bracing and rolling.

Fiberglass boats are extremely resistant to wear and tear. Because of their high durability, cruising on small, dangerous streams, full of more obstacles than water, is today's challenge, impossible before fiberglass. Scratches are repaired by adhesive tape; major damages, by resin and fiberglass. The high flexible strength of the thin shells renders stiff reinforcements of the bottom unnecessary and induces the craft to almost jump across obstructions. The rib free interior offers plenty of room for gear. In addition, a fiberglass boat can weather the elements well and can be stored outdoors if there is no other alternative.

Besides the one piece fiberglass boat, there are craft that can be broken down into sections. In this way, the advantages of the foldboat are nearly combined with those of the fiberglass.

Disadvantages: If the craft breaks in two, fiberglass splinters can cause

lacerations. Simultaneously, the paddler can be jammed inside the boat. If a fault exists in the construction of the boat, water pressure on the foredeck can collapse the craft, trapping the paddler. Safety breaking points need to be built into the craft behind the cockpit rim and perhaps in front of the foot brace. This would prevent the boat from breaking in two in the middle and trapping the paddler underwater. In addition, the boat would give way if it were jammed between boulders with the paddler pushed into the craft by the current. With such safety measures included in the design of fiberglass boats, many fatal accidents could have been prevented. Even after these considerations, a fiberglass boat is not as dangerous as a foldboat in boulder studded wild-water.

The fiberglass boat depends on the car for transportation. Consequently, it is more limited than the foldboat that can be carried by train, bus, mules. Because the fiberglass craft is nearly indestructible, it invites rougher handling than the fragile foldboat. As a result, it often has a shorter life span.

3. Open Inflated Boats

The open inflated boat is of great value particularly in expeditions and

as a sight-seeing craft. Unfortunately, it is often used by novices to tackle wild-water. In this way, accidents are nearly inevitable because of the lack of expertise of the boatman.

Construction

The construction of the inflated boat is based on the simple principle that air pressed into a container transforms the flexible container into a cylinder. This results in the greatest volume at the smallest surface. The primitive shape of the inflated boat consists of an oval tube with a bottom in between. The coated fabric is tear proof and airtight. Inflated boats are made in all sizes and variations, from the runabout to heavy robust boats suited for big water.

Advantages: The inflated boat has an enormous carrying capacity. Equipped with an outboard motor, it is suited for wild-water where kayak or canoe must give up. Even though such a situation does not exist in Europe, wild rivers in Canada and the United States seem to run forever with an overwhelming water volume. The inflated boat has many uses. It is a comfortable runabout and an expedition craft. A rope from stern to bow facilitates rescue actions and usage. Good nautical qualities are attributed to its round shape. Additional

airbags are not necessary. Lacking a rigid skeleton, it is insensitive to large waves. Sitting high on the side tubes, the boatman can paddle well. The paddler can abandon the craft easily when faced with an emergency. If it is broadsiding into trees, for example, the boatman can escape onto the obstacle. A damaged boat can be repaired without difficulty provided a repair kit is on board. The draft is low. Neither transportation nor stowing is a problem due to the small dimensions of the deflated boat. The simple construction of the inflated boat makes it attractive.

Disadvantages: The inflated boat is extremely sensitive to side wind. Its high resistance and friction behind dams and in rollers can cause a marked loss of speed and perhaps overturning. The craft is quickly slowed down and in big water there is no chance to prevent tipping over by bracing. As a consequence of the high resistance, rapid currents cannot be crossed easily. The open shape is often swamped in rough water, then resembling an inflatable bathtub. It is readily damaged by pointed objects. Within the boat, there is no support for the sitting or kneeling sportsman. Not without good reason, a British inflated-boat-expedition on the Blue Nile fastened a long line at

the stern by means of which participants who fell overboard could draw themselves back into the craft.

4. Covered Inflated Boats

This type of wild-water craft was first developed by the wild-water photographer and paddler, Hans Menninger, in cooperation with the Metzeler Company.

Construction

In principle, this boat resembles the open inflated craft. However, its wild-water suitability is markedly improved by an inflatable deck and a substantially narrower design with pronounced rocker.

Advantages: In heavy water, the boat rides smoother and drier than the rigid fiberglass craft. In roller waves and rapids, it performs well. With a larger volume, a wild-water inflated boat slips across spots which are crucial for a fiberglass craft. The fabric resists punctures as long as very sharp obstacles are avoided. The unrivaled positive aspects of the covered inflated boat are the flexibility, the simple and uncomplicated construction, and the small dimensions when deflated. It is particularly suited for use on rivers inaccessible

A covered wild-water inflated boat runs
the foaming back eddy of a heavy wild
river.

to rigid boats and unnavigable by foldboats.

Disadvantages: Because of the wider beam and the dissatisfying power transfer between body and boat, the wild-water inflated boat is difficult to roll and brace. The high resistance and friction entail problems when passing boulders and dams and when crossing and ferry gliding. All in all, the admittedly not very elegant wild-water inflated boat is unfairly judged with as much skepticism as were the first fiberglass boats. Perhaps the inflatables will do as much for the wild-water sport as fiberglass did. Logically, the constructive possibilities are not yet exhausted. Anyway, they represent the first true backpack boat!

5. Aluminium Boats

To complete the list, aluminum should be mentioned as a boat building material. It is of hardly any importance in the European wild-water sport. In the United States and Canada, however, aluminum canoes and rowboats run big water rivers.

Boat Weight

A fiberglass one-man wild-water kayak usually weighs 40 pounds (18 kg). But kayaks built for competition are as light as 16 to 18 pounds (7–8 kg). Fiberglass double canoes weigh about 55 pounds (25 kg) while open canoes are generally heavier at 60 to 90 pounds (30–40 kg).

By comparison, foldboats are light: 45 pounds (20 kg) for a one-man boat; 60 pounds (28 kg) for a double seater.

Inflated boats are light enough to be portaged distances without difficulty. They weigh in at about 30 pounds (15 kg) or more.

Seats

After considering the importance of foot and hip bracing in wild-water technique, the correct boat seat is as vital as the proper boat design. The seat cushions the paddler's lower back (kayak) and knees (canoe) against the force of turbulent water. It permits comfortable sitting without cramping the legs. In the one-man kayak, the seat is installed about 2 inches (5 cm) above the keel; in the double kayak, about 4 inches (10 cm);

and in the canoe, about 8 inches (20 cm). By meeting these wild-water construction requirements, the seat signals the paddler about the forces affecting the boat. In this way, the boater is warned seconds ahead of time that foot and hip bracing are needed to prevent capsizing. Simultaneously, the seat transfers to the boat the movements of the torso and the forces affecting the paddle. This is especially important when bracing the boat and when rolling. The seat should be affixed to the boat in such a way that it does not damage the hull in extremely rough water or when passing obstacles. Despite this perfectly firm seat, the paddler must always be able to leave the boat instantaneously in an emergency.

To guarantee a fast, safe exit, certain devices need to be built into the canoe or kayak. In canoes, for example, there are devices which fall out under emergency conditions to facilitate abandoning the boat. There are also comfortable, functional seat belts, saddle-like designs, and knee pads made of foam rubber.

The kayak seat is sometimes built in a one piece design with the hip brace or it can be supplemented by a back belt. When purchasing a boat, attention should be paid to a sufficient forward opening of the hip braces and

a seat angle that permits the paddler the necessary forward lean. Upper thighs and knees are supported in the kayak by devices like tubes, boards, or extra elevation in the deck. The more the knees can be straddled, the more power the paddler can exert in propelling the craft.

Foot braces can be made of aluminum or fiberglass. They are adjustable and affixed laterally. There exists a variety of designs. However, they should be absolutely resistant to breakage and should assist the paddler in maintaining control. In rollers powerful enough to flatten the craft, foot braces could drop out of the boat unless secured on both sides.

Only a few types of boats on the market today have seats that meet the recommended requirements. But a skilled do-it-yourself man can fashion an excellent seat for every type of white-water craft. With a fiberglass boat, a saw, file, and repair kit may be needed for the job. The wild-water boat must be equipped with a cockpit rim. Its shape should permit sufficient space in rolling (backward lean) and perfect but not too tight fastening of the sprayskirt (see section "Sea Training – Fastening the Sprayskirt"). Chamfered cockpit rims are the rule today: they are not as easily torn off in the event of over-

turning and turbulent water does not splash off of them into the eyes of the boatman.

The kayak seat has the following dimensions: width, 15 inches (38 cm); the measurement of the cockpit rim is 28 inches (70 cm). The canoe seat is 15 inches (38 cm) wide with a cockpit rim of 24 inches (60 cm). Once the measurements in kayak building become standard, sprayskirts can be interchanged. Loops also should be built into the wild-water craft. They facilitate rescue actions and portage. The wider they are, the handier.

The bow deck on nearly all wild-water boats is too weak. The danger is that the water pressure of heavy rapids will trap the paddler. A deck on which you can stand without deforming it would be the safest.

Flotation

Foldboats and fiberglass craft used in wild-water should be protected from sinking and breakage by air bags (see the section "Sea Training – Emptying the Boat"). Flotation bags come in different lengths. Never use bags shorter than 4 feet (120 cm), because they would prove too small in an emergency.

A wild-water single kayak contains about 12 cubic feet (350 liters) of air. A 4 cubic foot (100 liter) buoyancy still leaves nearly 600 pounds (270 kg) worth of swamped boat (water weighs over 8 pounds per gallon). Insert the flotation bags in bow and stern to achieve horizontal trim and reduce the danger of damage. Secure the bags to the inside of the craft.

Double canoes and double kayaks are particularly wearisome to rescue because of their high volume. The air bags normally offered for the central part of the craft are insufficient. Instead, huge flotation bags should be installed at bow and stern. The conventional flotation bags should not be pulled out of the boat by the hose because it either rips or tears off as a result.

The safety bag is more effective than any other type of flotation. It is a watertight bag affixed at the cockpit rim and the foot braces. The paddler sits in it. The sprayskirt is fastened above as usual. After capsizing, only about 20 gallons (80 liters) of water maximum will swamp the boat. Depending on the boat's volume, around 10 cubic feet (300 liters) of air will remain in the boat.

Tears in the flotation bags can be patched with plastic cement. An air pump is also recommended.

Paddles

The paddle propels, stops, turns, and moves the canoe or kayak laterally. The boater uses it to brace the craft and keep it from overturning. And it is an integral part of the Eskimo roll. The paddle should be free to move in all directions and not locked to the hull as is the case with rowboats. The double paddle propels the kayak. The single paddle guides the canoe with the paddler seated as high as possible (12 to 14 inches) while floating smooth water and kneeling when negotiating wild-water. The position of the boater helps him get maximal effectiveness from his strokes.

The more stable, one piece paddle is used in wild-water floating. The shaft consists of pine reinforced with ash. For racing, the paddle is hollow, achieving lightweight. In all cases, the shafts are no longer circular as in former times but show an elliptical cross section which facilitates blade control in drawing and rolling. Paddle blades differ markedly in shape and curvature. In wild-water paddling, the curvature used successfully in slalom competition became the standard, that is, about 3/4 inch (2 cm) in length with cross spooning of about 1/10 inch (.3 cm). The stronger the curvature and spooning,

the greater is the bite of the blade in the water.

However, wild-water boaters discovered that maximum bite is less important than suitability for drawing and rolling. This requires a markedly curved blade that is only slightly spooned. Strongly spooned blades create a narrow curve when slicing the water. Flat blades have the lowest bite in wild-water.

When purchasing paddles, be certain that the blades do not flutter in the water when pulled vigorously. Like the shaft, the blades are usually made of pine with the tips reinforced by hardwood or cross veneer. In kayak racing, laminated blades are preferred but the synthetics are now entering paddle production, usually in the form of resin impregnated fiberglass with a Duraluminum shaft. The blade shape is almost bottle-like with straight tips.

Usually the blade size of the kayak paddle is about 8 inches (20 cm) by 20 inches (48 cm). The blade of the canoe paddle measures 8 inches (20 cm) by 24 inches (60 cm).

When choosing a paddle, pick one that is the correct length and either right- or left-handed (see the section "Training – Paddling without Boat"). The optimum paddle length for wild-water kayaking is when the blade tip,

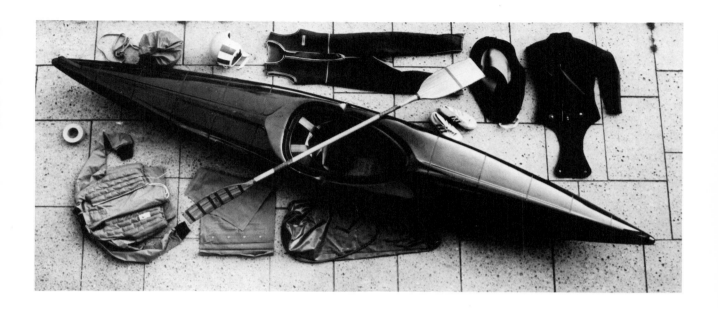

in a vertical position, reaches to the middle of the standing paddler's stretched hand. If the paddler is 5 feet 9 inches tall, the paddle length would be 6 feet 9 inches. The length of the canoe paddle is a proper fit if it can easily be held at grip and tip with the arms outstretched.

With the proper length paddle, the closer the blade is moved alongside the boat and the more vertically it is inserted, the higher is its efficiency (see section "Training – Paddling Forward in Kayak and Canoe").

By increasing stroke frequency, the paddler is more alert physically and mentally, is a safer boater, and is more attuned to the river. At the same time, the boat can better be accelerated as is best demonstrated by a comparison with a racing cyclist who achieves better acceleration at high speed. Performance is the product of a force acting through a given distance in a given unit of time. The physically weak paddler, who often is a lightweight person as well, can achieve the same performance of a physically strong and heavier paddler by high stroke frequency and shorter paddle length. The conclusion to be drawn from this theory is that many wild-water touring paddlers have paddles that are much too long. Perhaps the Eskimos reached the same conclusion and came to use relatively short paddles and small blades.

Sprayskirts

The first sprayskirts were used by the Eskimos, who originated wild-water cruising. The sprayskirt of the Eskimos was an anorak fitted around the circular tiny manhole. This design works well today.

The sprayskirt is made of waterproof fabric and is worn around the waist. A drawstring fits the skirt snugly to the boater. A shock cord sewn into the bottom opening of the skirt hugs the cockpit rim and is secured by the paddler in the seated position. The skirt keeps spray and water from entering the cockpit. In the event of a hasty exit from the boat, the shock cord attachment pulls free from the rim and does not entrap the paddler.

A spray cover is a larger version of the sprayskirt. It is a cover for the open canoe which keeps boat and cargo dry in rough water and bad weather. There must be at least one loop at the front end of the spray cover to facilitate removal. In former times, spray covers were made of robust, coated canvas. Canoeists were the first to make spray covers that were neoprene coated on both sides. Today the double coated sprayskirt is the rule with most kayakers and canoeists because of its durability and the better fit to the cockpit rim and to the paddler's body. Thus, the suspenders on the sprayskirts of years ago which often tore off during the Eskimo roll have been adequately replaced.

Occasionally, one piece spray covers are offered for open double kayaks and canoes, where the manhole is closed around the body. This type of spray cover is dangerous and completely unsuited for wild-water cruising because rapid exiting after capsizing is not always possible.

Repair Kit

The wild-water paddler should carry along a repair kit. A roll of broad textile adhesive tape can repair many defects of boat and paddle as well as tears in tent or down sleeping bag. Tweezers are of importance in removing fiberglass slivers from the inside of the boat or from damaged parts.

Repair more serious damage with fiberglass and resin. The resin to be used, particularly for river bank repair, should be catalyzed to such a degree that it hardens within one hour. For prolonged cruising under severe conditions, 2 pounds (1 kg) of resin and 1 square yard (1 m²) of fiberglass cloth per boat and week should be sufficient. In addition, the paddler should have a suitable hardener, a flat brush, and a rasp. Foldboat and inflated boat paddlers should obtain patching material prior to the trip. Follow the repair instructions of the manufacturer.

Repair and Care

Compared to the foldboat, the fiberglass boat seems nearly indestructible. Even though it can tolerate rather brutal handling, wild-water makes its mark on the bottom of the boat over several summers. The entire surface will most likely be scratched. The stern will be dotted with tears and white spots. The bow will be gouged with small pieces missing.

This wear and tear results from mishandling rather than defects in fiberglass. But as a result, the boat will ride less easily and be less turnable. Breaks and tears should be patched carefully with subsequent sanding and puttying.

A foldboater would never think of dragging his dearly acquired boat over gravel down to the wild-water stream. He would not slide it across dry dams nor leave the boat for weeks in the garden, exposed to the elements. But fiberglass owners believe their boats should require no special treatment.

If you want to preserve the extraordinary wild-water suitability of your modern boat, its maneuverability, swiftness, and easy run, you must handle it with kid gloves. Then it survives broadsiding a boulder better than a craft that is mishandled.

A cared-for boat is not only easier to paddle, it is also more reliable and therefore safer in emergencies.

With regard to care, do not expose the brand-new boat immediately to the utmost strain. It gets its final rigidity and elasticity only in the course of several weeks. The outer surface of the craft is best protected by a coating of floor wax which reduces surface friction and susceptibility to scratches. The inner surface of the boat sucks up water if not treated with a preservative. Be careful not to deform the lower shell of the boat when stowing and transporting. A rocker that is reduced or pressed inward would make the boat slower and less maneuverable. A sponge is rather indispensable because a sponge soaks up the water that is impossible to empty after swamping a boat. Every boat should be completely dried as soon as the trip is finished. The air bags prevent drying and should be removed from the boat during storage.

As mentioned in the section "Repair Kit," textile adhesive tape can handle many small emergency repairs to canoes and kayaks. The spots to be repaired must be dry. It also can protect the boat, reduce damage, and cut down on the amount of water taken in. Before a trip where heavy water and many obstacles are anticipated, cover the stern with textile adhesive tape. Or you can redress defects of the craft with tape, as long as the inherent stability remains. Eventually, you will have to work with fiberglass and resin. Roughen the defect with a rasp (not a file) or a suitable type of sandpaper. Remove wax residue by benzine. Put three torn patches of fiberglass differing in size one after the other onto the dry spot and saturate them with resin. The method is applicable both inside and out. Both-side patching is best. Often, however, it is possible only from the outside. Sand the rough surface and putty it.

After a while, paddle blades show thin longitudinal tears. Repair them by gluing with kauri resin dissolved in hardener. Bend and release the tears so that the glue sucks in. Finally, tape the blade.

Tips: Paddles reinforced by elastic tape at the tips and with a few cross strips stand more wear. If the blade breaks, the individual parts won't drift away.

Foam rubber cushions underneath the seat eliminate the seat bumping the bottom of the boat in rough water. Remove them before storing the craft.

Do-It-Yourself Equipment

Do-it-yourself boats are built to save money and to create the ideal wild-water craft. If successful boats are not simply to be copied, you must design a boat and build a mold of your own. To make a mold takes about 300 hours of work. From the mold, a so-called negative is formed. The processing of fiberglass and resin is dealt with so widely in the literature provided by the producers that a detailed description is not necessary in this context. Information not contained in the literature will be briefly summarized in the following:

● Provided the boat will have to stand normal strain, three layers of fiberglass fabric will be sufficient for the bottom. Diolen is an effective reinforcing fabric. At the stern, middle, and bow, several layers can be patched one over the other.

● The deck is made of 2 layers of fiberglass cloth; the middle, of 3 layers. The part around the cockpit rim down to the foot braces should be reinforced by a third layer. A roofed deck does not require further reinforcement. In case of a flat deck, ribs made of doubled

This C 2 passes a difficult roller wave. Note the helmet, sleeveless neoprene tunic and sprayskirt which are indispensable in wild-water cruising.

strips of fabric are inserted every foot (30 cm) or so.

- Seat and cockpit rim consist of 4 layers of fabric. The seat is affixed to the deck before bottom and deck are put together. This is best achieved by short cut rowing ropes which will be laminated into the gap between cockpit rim and deck.

- The beveled half shells are obtusely patched together by means of elastic tape or similar material. A pointed screwdriver or a short knife can help you to adjust the shells exactly to each other. Now, set the boat on edge. On a Resopal plate then saturate 4-inch (10 cm) strips of fiberglass, one third the length of the boat, with resin. Roll them up and out again inside the boat. Attach these strips to a precise fixed point in order to avoid surplus material in bow and stern. Use a large brush to smooth and squeeze the air bubbles out of the seam. For the seam itself, 2 layers of fabric are sufficient.

- With careful processing, a finished 13-foot (4 m) boat, built according to the above information, will weigh about 40 pounds (18 kg).

- For extremely light slalom boats or wild-water racing kayaks, the bottom may have only one layer of fabric with Diolen reinforcement.

The deck can be built with only one layer of fabric with massive reinforcement in the cockpit region.

- The most expensive surface protection of the hull is laminated gel resin which must be hardened before the shells are made. The cheapest material is simple resin which is suited for immediate further processing. The best solution is polyester fleece which is processed with laminated resin too. Further processing is possible before the hardening process is finished.

- Flat brushes can be cleaned easily.

- Small (4-inch diameter), Teflon rollers and rollers made of Perlon are best for squeezing out air bubbles from the laminate.

- Fiberglass dust produces itching and should be avoided as much as possible.

- A spectacular boat color facilitates every rescue action.

- Do not forget to install the foot braces prior to joining bottom with the deck. A boat without foot braces is dangerous. Inexpensive foot braces are broad Perlon belts screwed into the boat.

Clothing

A life vest should be worn at all times. It is important to use a U.S. Coast Guard approved life vest for wild-water cruising. Most vests sold in stores today are Coast Guard approved and are acceptable for a variety of water sports. However, the choice and fitting of a wild-water vest are extremely important. It should be trim and snug-fitting with freedom of movement. Even though it is easier to perform the Eskimo roll without wearing a life vest, mastery of the roll is not complete until it can be executed while wearing one. A life jacket facilitates swimming in heavy water and improves orientation. It protects the body from collisions and helps counteract the paralyzing effect of frigid water. If the paddler is unconscious, the vest facilitates rescue action by companions.

For good reason, the crash helmet was made compulsory for wild-water races. Running wild-water full of rapids and submerged rocks involves the danger of head injuries in the event of capsizing. In addition to helmets developed especially for wild-water sports, skiers' helmets are being used frequently. They fit better, are warmer, and protect larger parts of the forehead and neck. When you

Eskimo roll, hardly any water penetrates the helmet. Bright colors increase safety by making the paddler more visible.

Among wild-water paddlers, the skin diver's wet suit is becoming standard equipment. Made of neoprene, it increases by tenfold the immersion time a boater can safely be in the water without danger of hypothermia. Coated material is preferred because of its longer service life. The tunic has a special piece of cloth that fits between the legs and fastens in front. This flap prevents the jacket from riding up and exposing the torso to cold water and abrasions.

At times, the snug-fitting wet suit interferes with paddling and can be unpleasantly hot under a glaring sun. By wearing both the neoprene pants and tunic, buoyancy is increased, however, there are disputes among the experts concerning whether or not the complete wet suit should be worn. In racing, the pants are worn with a life vest. A sweater – an old cashmere is best – can be worn under the wet suit to prevent possible allergic reaction.

The author prefers a wet suit with a sleeveless tunic, orange or yellow coated on both sides. In cold weather, a neoprene jacket supplements the outfit and has a smooth, tightly fitting collar. In addition, both the vest and the jacket should have a breast belt and a covered ring inserted for rescue actions. The boater should wear boots over neoprene socks. They protect the feet from sharp-edged boulders, tree limbs, and broken glass. They also facilitate portage in rough terrain. Rubber boots can be lost in a turbulent current. Watertight mountaineer's boots are recommended.

Spare clothing should be carried in a pack. After a long wild-water trip, warm clothing is absolutely necessary despite a neoprene wet suit. Pure wool will insure warmth even if it is wet whereas synthetic fiber and cotton are ineffective. Neoprene gloves or ski gloves protect the hands from cold but they should be tested prior to a trip.

In a pack with extra clothes store camera, film, food, and a first aid kit.

Loading

Each kayaker has his own ideas about how to load his one-man boat for an extended wild-water trip. But there are certain basic rules to follow to keep the boat suited for wild-water cruising.

Every boat is designed for a defined center of gravity. The paddler's weight determines trim. As a consequence, the packs should be distributed in the craft to maintain normal trim. Remember that maneuverability is least affected when added weight is concentrated near the center of gravity. This enables the boat to pivot and ride rapids without hindrance. In a double canoe, proper weight distribution is no problem. The huge space amidships can take more gear than probably needed. Contrary to former practice, stow heavy packs around, under, or just behind the seat of the kayak. Lightweight articles are stashed in the bow and stern, if necessary. They can remain in the boat during a difficult portage. The rest of the gear should be packed into watertight backpacks. They can be slipped onto the back for portaging. All packs should be secured to the boat to prevent loss in the event of capsizing. Having loose bags rumbling around inside the boat can disturb a kayaker during his Eskimo roll. The seats of foldboat kayaks are left home for a wild-water trip. A storage bag can double as a seat in order for the paddler to sit higher and have more clearance for his paddle.

Storage

The individual boater stores his craft in the garage or back yard turned up-

side down, resting on two sawhorses. Foldboats and inflated wild-water boats can be stowed wherever space is available. However, the manufacturer's recommendations should be kept in mind. Store boats in such a way that they will not bend out of shape over a period of time. Foldboats survive the winter best assembled and protected from moisture, severe cold, and intense heat. Fiberglass boats should be stored in a similar way with safeguards against warping and damage caused by extreme temperatures.

Transport

Being able to transport the fiberglass boat on the top of a car has been responsible for the popularity of the wild-water sports. Because fiberglass can be damaged by abrasions, protect the boats from metal cartop racks, protruding screws, and from rubbing against each other. Rubber, plastic or foam pads should cushion the boats in transit.

How to arrange boats on a cartop:

● Put boats on edge. In this way, they are less likely to be bent out of shape and take up less room. Four boats can then be transported simultaneously.

● Boats laid flat on the cartop carrier should be secured with the cockpit upside down and the bow facing backward. As a result, rain will run off of the boat and wind resistance will be reduced.

● By covering the cockpit with a tied up sprayskirt, air resistance will be reduced.

If the weight of the boats exceeds the recommended cartop carrying capacity, use a trailer. It is easy to load and unload and enables the gear to be stored inside the boats. Speed with such a trailer should not exceed 45 mph but cartop carrying also requires self-restraint in this respect.

The transport of one piece paddles sometimes requires special consideration. Long boats offer sufficient space for the paddles but frequently the shaft is damaged by the rear edge of the seat. Paddles can be tied between the boats. Make sure, however, that the paddles never touch the metal carrier which would impair the wood, blacking spots that would break later on. Many paddles break not because of instability but because of mishandling during transport.

Railway transport of wild-water boats is time consuming and troublesome. Many put-in points can be reached only after a long march from the railway station with a boat cart. The boat

cart can be useful on other trips too. The Upper Isar in the Karwendel Mountains is out of reach to car traffic because the access road is closed. Typical of this type of wild-water trip, you pack all equipment and gear onto the boat cart, walk for two hours through the mountains and have lunch. Finally, you run the rapids back through the magnificent gorges. The detachable boat cart can be packed inside the smallest of wild-water kayaks.

Costs

White-water cruising can be both an expensive and cheap sport. Expensive, because the equipment costs as much as top-notch ski equipment. Cheap, because clothing is not yet subject to fashion crazes. Cheap, because boat, paddle, and clothes will last at least five summers with careful handling. Expensive, because the car is the only means of transporting the boat to the river, unless you want to use the folding bicycle or the boat cart for your trips. Cheap, because you are propelled cost-free by the current.

Hardly any vacation or weekend is spent as simply with as much fun as that of the wild-water paddler's Far

This European river offers the wild-water boater a variety of challenges.

away from camping fees and civilization. No neon signs nor portable radios. No slamming doors nor disruptive revelers coming home after a night on the town.

Cost of Equipment:	
Wild-water boat	$ 300
Paddle, double	$ 40
Paddle, single	$ 20
Life vest	$ 25
Helmet	$ 20
Sprayskirt	$ 30
Spray cover	$ 175
Flotation bag	$ 16
Wet suit, pants	$ 55
Wet suit, tunic	$ 60
Wet suit, boots	$ 18
Wet suit, mitts	$ 15
Waterproof cargo bag	$ 10
Cartop carrier	$ 38

Even though the cost seems high, you will receive a much higher degree of enjoyment. In short, it's worth the money. You can paddle anywhere. Your contact with nature is intimate. You will meet people stream-side with similar values and interests as yours. You can save money if you build the boat yourself. However, this pays off only if you have a contract with a boys club, for example, to make ten boats for them. Otherwise the ex-

pense for a design and mold is much too high. With ten do-it-yourself boats, the cost will be one-third of the selling price. By the way, manufacturers sometimes grant quantity discounts and winter prices.

The secondhand boat is the cheapest solution. By scouting for a used boat among canoe or kayak club members, you will undoubtedly find a suitable boat. However, never choose a fragile, edged competition boat. You will always have trouble with such a craft. Ask an experienced wild-water paddler to accompany you on your search for a boat. Be certain of sufficient clearance in the back (see section "Eskimo Roll") and firm but comfortable sitting. The bottom should always be colorless. The finest coat of varnish can cover the largest number of decayed spots that can cause breaks in the near future. All bright colors are suitable for the deck.

Robust paddles with plastic blades and aluminum shafts are occasionally the handiwork of a do-it-yourselfer. When shopping for wet suits, allow for swelling of the muscles when being measured for the tunic and pants. Crash helmets, mountaineering helmets, ice hockey helmets, a large variety of equipment is available that can be used for wild-water floating. The hull of a do-it-yourself foldboat

needs to be sewn by a company with a specialized machine, one designed for such a job.

Types of Current

Wild-water is always a sign of fast water and high gradient which presents many difficulties to the floater.

◄ This V-shaped gorge is characteristic of rivers in an early developmental stage.

A magazine article about an inflated boat expedition in Africa contained the following sentence: "When we were drawn into a rapid all steering became useless. We could do nothing but hope not to be capsized." The wild-water expert is surprised. Or is it rather the view of an individual who never studied river morphology? For him everything is a whirlpool that turns, foams, or looks strange in one way or the other.

Herbert Rittlinger writes with good reason: "The kayakist blind to the character of his element would be a bad friend of nature and a still worse kayak man." The novice who unsuspectingly runs into the mirrored return eddy and disappears after capsizing is forced by the wild-water to study the natural laws by which every river is governed.

The surface of the earth was formed by water. Civilization followed water. In each mountain valley, you can see the villages founded on top of the alluvial cones of the side valleys.

Forced by the rhythm of the floods, the Mesopotamians ("land between the rivers") and Egyptians started to calculate the sequence of the seasons. They began planning and contributed to the basis of the present civilization. It seems, however, that nowadays the relationship between

water and civilization is no longer recognized by most of mankind. The wild-water paddler is a friend of nature. Every river bank fascinates him. He can recognize how water, weighing over 8 pounds per gallon, continuously saws the land into individual plateaus. Water flows downhill. Nobody can hinder it. If dammed, it looks for another channel. It pushes all obstacles out of the way.

Seen scientifically, every river runs through four stages if not altered by man-made obstructions or natural events. In its infancy, it rushes through steep, V-shaped gorges down into the valley, piling up huge alluvial cones wherever it releases energy. Falls, boulders, and sharp-edged rocks determine the topography. To the wild-water paddler, this part of the river is of little interest. To the hiker, however, it offers the best drinking water. The closer to the valley, the more the water disappears underground. Except when flooding, as during a thaw or violent thunderstorm, the river bed dries up.

In its youth, the slope of the river is gentler and attracts many advanced wild-water paddlers. As a torrent, the water plunges across huge boulders forming foaming whirlpools or souse holes full of wild water. At these spots, the water rotates back so that

the kayaker-canoeist has to fight to get his boat out of the return eddy. When capsized, he encounters difficulties in rolling. If he must abandon his craft, he should not rush to the surface immediately because the back-flowing water would seize and hold him until he is pushed downward again by the water dropping from above. This requires breath and nerve.

In the middle of the tongue of the current, the water runs at the highest speed. There are huge boulders which repel water and form vehement cross currents. As a result of the turbulence, the water excavates the ground in front of the boulder, forming a deep pool which directs the current more forcibly to the obstacle. One day the boulder will finally be removed. Behind the boulder, the water is relatively quiet. It rises from below like a flat boil yet rotates simultaneously making a big whirlpool. The paddler swings his boat into this eddy. The eddy pushes the boat upstream and again to the tongue of the current. Here are funnel-shaped vortexes which dissipate as they go downstream.

With little water volume, these whirlpools can draw the paddle of an inexperienced boater under the water surface. With a lot of water, the boater feels he is swimming inside his craft. If capsized in a whirlpool, the wild-water paddler postpones rolling until the boat no longer rotates. If you must abandon the boat, hold onto it or dive down and break away laterally. A powerful swimmer may even stroke his way through large whirlpools.

From the return eddy the wild-water paddler can often get a good view of the stretch ahead. He might also be able to see the nearest return eddy he can safely reach. In this way, he may run a dangerous wild-water river according to the relatively safe method "from return eddy to return eddy."

Sometimes the river disappears from the field of vision. The water surface seems to be cut off. Such passages must be inspected. With a considerable drop in grade, the water dashes over three-foot high rapids, forming deep foaming holes. Even though these cataracts can be negotiated (though with great difficulty) it would be absurd to decide from the boat the suitable route through a labyrinth of rocks.

Suddenly easy wild-water becomes a very difficult cataract.

Study the photo as if you expected to run this stretch momentarily. Note the waterfall, a short rivulet, the steep outside bend.

Occasionally passage is barred by rock jams. Water passes under the jams without a return eddy, much like through a siphon. It is unlikely you could recognize such a siphon ahead of time from the boat. In case of collision, you and the boat would be drawn under the rock, where survival would be doubtful. You would either have to counterbalance the current or dive through the obstacle without

being trapped by branches or rock edges. Behind the siphon, the water boils. Under such circumstances, it is best to portage.

In certain narrow bends of the river, the current runs directly toward the outside of the turn. Floating debris sometimes accumulates at such spots. Unless you are alert, the current will take you into the debris. To

capsize there could be fatal (see section "Rescue Methods").

Where tributaries broaden the river, a pool is formed at their junction followed by haystacks down to the next pool. The diagonal crests of waves get larger and larger at the foot of the V-shaped haystacks and the velocity is continuously increasing. Some haystacks have such a gradient that it is difficult to make out their exact

Behold wild-water pleasure at its finest: high waves and foaming rollers.

course from the boat. The experienced paddler drifts down slowly, ready to swing into an eddy if a rapid would suddenly appear. High roller waves should be inspected closely before you run them. You must take them at high speed with perfect technique (see section "Training in the Roller Wave"). Furthermore, you never know whether the haystacks will end in a cataract. You can easily pass the pointed waves of haystacks. At times they may curl back upstream or end in foaming breakers which are usually not dangerous.

High round waves, on the other hand, can hide boulders. Behind these, souse holes can cause problems. With increasing water volume, the back eddy of souse holes and whirlpools becomes stronger. At the foot of steep haystacks which plunge into a wide, slow flowing pool, rollers of vast dimensions are sometimes observed. These haystacks are frequently accompanied by cross-rollers beginning before the eddies. In the bend of the river, steep haystacks followed by many cross-rollers are difficult to negotiate. Because the cross-rollers are thrown back from the outside bank of the bend, the boater should ride them crosswise (athwart). The steeper the banks, the stronger are the overlapping waves. Where the river is hemmed in by a cliff wall, the cross currents, the side eddies, and the boilers emerging from a deep pool are indeed bewildering. However, there is usually little danger. A capsize near the wall will push the boater forward rapidly. The expert would remain in the boat and roll a little later.

Walls that are hollowed out or partially eroded away by the current do not generate cross currents. But instead, strong swelling boilers take over and are nearly as dangerous as the siphon. Shun the hollowed out wall without panic by applying the right tactics. After a capsize, when you cannot stay afloat, dive deeply with the current which resurfaces again near the boilers.

A gorge is a steep sloping bank on

Most difficult wild-water: haystacks in high water; a smooth tongue of the current ending in a narrow V and followed by a series of huge cross-rollers.

both sides of the river. Portage is rough but sometimes possible without climbing out of the gorge.

A rock wall that drops vertically into the water and jams the river is a canyon, glen, or ravine. Escape from a canyon can be made only by climbing out. This can become dangerous if an unnavigable and fatal stretch blocks the river. An alternative way to escape from a canyon would be to run the upstream eddies of the river where the tongue of the current would have to be crossed only occasionally. Herbert Rittlinger escaped by this method when he pioneered the Upper Amazon.

Extremely high or low water could make a navigable stretch impassable.

During flood stage, the river can level the valley by swinging in vast bends from one side of the valley to the other where it rebounds off a hard slope, goes in the opposite direction and rebounds again. Wherever it loses speed, boulders, gravel, sand, and mud are deposited. These are the places where the paddler portages.

Low water makes it difficult for the kayaker to find the naviagble channel. The roaring rapids requires the boatman's attention. Side channels branch off so suddenly that the proper course is lost. At times, you will float a stream that dead-ends. Then, a portage to the main channel is necessary. Usually the current with

the coarser gravel and the deeper water is the best.

Along the outside of the bends, the river is obviously deeper because speed and erosive power are greater.

The water spirals downhill. Pressed outward by centrifugal force, it flows fastest near the outside bank but returns in the eddy. At the same time, the water is pressed upward forming as cross currents from the outside bank and boilers in the eddy at the end of the spiral movements. The current differentials of cross current, tongue current, and eddy, drag the boat to and fro, turn the stern downstream, or careen the boat away from one stable direction.

In high water, floating trees and flooded, overgrown islets can be dangerous (see section "Recue Methods"). With increasing water volume and gradient, the turbulent wild-water becomes more difficult to negotiate. In addition, overlapping waves intensify the complexity of the currents from the banks, obstacles, and eddies.

In the old age stage, the kinetic energy of rivers is reduced by friction in the river bed and within the water (silt), by decreasing gradient, and by slowing down at bends to such an extent that debris accumulates where the current is slowest.

The wild-water paddler must be prepared to portage around unnavigable water.

In this way, the river increasingly obstructs its own way. As a result, the river branches, forming islets and numerous channels which become independent. If debris blocks the inflow of the channel, it becomes dead.

A large meandering river flows through countryside largely leveled in the course of millenniums. This peaceful setting can be changed, however, if the river breaks over its boundaries and once again erodes the land as in its youth.

A completely new process of erosion now begins in the stretch of river with the highest gradient. The erosion continues upstream so that the river sets out to cut to pieces the valley land already leveled. The erosive

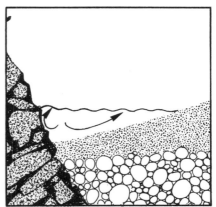

Section of a bend in a river.

A wild river in the Alps. Free and unregulated; neither dammed nor diverted.

force of the mature river is directed horizontally. But for this rejuvenated river, downcutting becomes the principal type of erosive power. This leads to gorges of unique beauty, often narrow like a glen. At the flanks of the valley, you can sometimes recognize the former, deeply scratched out undercut slopes high above. If the river meets softer strata, the bends become larger and such formations result as the famous Pont D'Arc of the Ardeche in the Provence where the river broke through the outside slope and formed a huge door in the mountain. The same process can be initiated by the elevation of the ground as was the case with the Grand Canyon of the Colorado River.

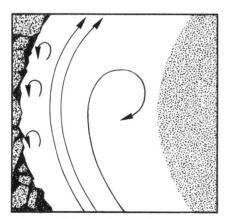

Top view of the bend in the river.

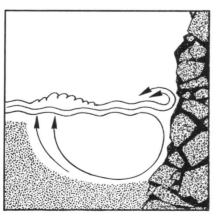

Cliff wall

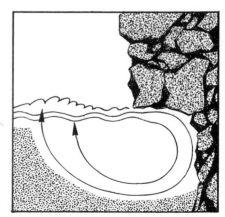

Undercut wall

Of unique beauty and unspeakable peace, floating a river.

Such rivers tend more easily to hollow out the outside bank of a turn. Or, they break through subterraneously. Rivers running through chalky plateaus also tend to hollow out the bank. But besides erosion by mechanical influences, the water dissolves the ground by chemical processes as well.

In addition to many natural obstacles, the wild-water paddler also has to be alert to man-made ones. Whereas natural obstacles are subject to defined laws and have a distinct character, man's artifacts are not.

Wooden bridges may bar passage during high water. Heaps of driftwood accumulate around bridge abutments. Discarded wire and cable are particularly treacherous. In the upper courses in V-shaped gorges, steep concrete weirs threaten to drown the paddler in the back eddy below the weir's lip. The only safeguard is maximum precaution: prior inspection in all cases and portage if necessary. Besides leftover obstructions and trees fallen across the dam, shallow water behind the dam can be dangerous. The foot brace may break if the craft bumps the river bottom and jam the paddler inside the boat. Box-like, concrete dams are particularly troublesome because of their long foaming back eddy. Drops from

the upper to the lower level are commonly fatal because of the underwater construction directly below the dam. From the days when logs were rafted down river, there exists dams with raft channels which you can frequently ride – but inspect them first to make sure. Subterranean tunnels and underwater floodgates are fatal to the boater. In both cases, the river is artificially diverted through subterranean constructions.

In gravel beds, piles and collapsed bridges are often surprises to the wild-water paddler that could cost him his boat, if not his life. These inconspicuous narrow obstructions do not generate a strong back eddy as do natural ones. Instead of using them for a necessary escape from rough water, the artificially induced back eddy catches the broadsiding boat, breaks it in two, and jams the paddler.

Furthermore, iron girders are dangerous. If a collision is unavoidable, abandon the boat as quickly as possible shortly before it broadsides by jumping on top of the obstruction.

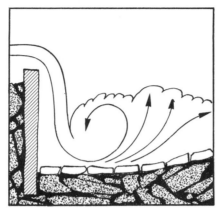

Section through a vertical dam with roller-topped eddy.

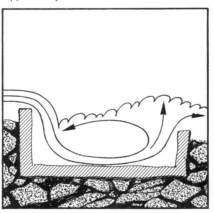

Section through a box-like dam with roller-topped eddy.

To negotiate a dam of nearly 10 feet, the water below the dam must be deep enough.

River Ratings

A difficulty rating system is used in the wild-water sport to give the paddler an idea of the forthcoming difficulties. This involves the problem of how to meet the completely differing characters of wild rivers with water volume on the one hand and boulder fields on the other in one and the same difficulty rating classification. The American Wild-Water Affiliation has established a river rating system that can be used as a general reference.

Class I – Very Easy

For the practiced beginner. Waves are small and regular. Passages are clear. Usually gentle sand or dirt banks, with some possible artificial difficulties like bridge abutments or a few small riffles.

Class II – Easy

For intermediates. Rapids are of medium difficulty. Passages are clear and wide. Some low ledges. Spray covers might be useful. Some maneuvering is required.

Class III – Medium Difficult

For experienced boaters. There are numerous high, irregular waves. There are rocks, eddies, and rapids with passages that are clear, though they can be narrow and require expertise in maneuvering. Inspection before making the run is necessary in some areas, and sprayskirt or splash cover is necessary.

Class IV – Difficult

For highly skilled boaters with several years of experience. Should be with an organized group of boaters for this run. There are long rapids and powerful, irregular waves. Dangerous rocks and boiling eddies are common. Passages are difficult. Inspection is a must. Powerful and precise maneuvering is required and sprayskirt or splash cover is essential. Conditions along these stretches make rescue difficult in case of trouble and all kayakers should be able to Eskimo roll.

Class V – Very Difficult

For teams of experts, having extremely long, difficult and violent rapids that follow each other almost without interruption. Plenty of obstacles, big drops, violent current, and very steep gradient. Shore scouting and planning is essential, but extremely difficult because of the terrain. Because rescue conditions on this stretch are extremely difficult, mishaps can and do often lead to death.

Class VI – Extremely Difficult

For teams of experts. Nearly impossible to run and very dangerous. Even for teams of experts, favorable water levels and close study and careful planning are needed for success. When judging difficulty ratings, remember that they differ from country to country. A French Class IV corresponds to a German Class V and an American Class VI. In addition, the ratings vary markedly with changes in water level. The river bed of a white-water section alters from flood to flood and from year to year. Prior inspection of difficult water is recommended.

Rescue Methods

Capsize cannot be avoided. It belongs in training because a calculated risk must be part of the learning process. It is an integral part of whitewater trips because miscalculations cannot be eliminated.

Salvage of Your Own Boat in Haystacks

Keep the keel of the overturned craft in an upward position. Hold the boat by the loop and align it to the current. In shallow water, find a secure foothold and jump or swim into the nearest eddy, pushing or dragging the boat. The inside eddy of a bend takes more time to reach but guarantees a softer landing and easier emptying of the boat. It also is easier to get back into the boat and shove off from there. The eddy on the outside of a turn can be reached quickly but causes a rougher landing and more difficulty in emptying the boat and starting again.
If the river is broad, try creeping onto the stern.

Problems

● The boat turns over several times and is swamped with water.
● The cockpit of the boat is exposed to the current.
● The boater grabs the boat in the middle.

Information on how to empty a boat is given in the section "Training, Emptying the Boat."

Salvage of the Boat in Blocked Water

Prevent the boat from being jammed between the rocks by a strong current. To do this, raise one end of the boat by the loop and align the boat to the current. Turn the cockpit down river to prevent further swamping. Empty the boat in the next eddy if attempts to reach shore with the swamped boat would be perilous.

Problems

● The boatman is caught between obstacle and boat, which is dangerous, possibly fatal.
● The boatman pulls the boat toward himself instead of vice versa to get a better position.
● The cockpit of the boat is turned across the current.

Salvage of a Boat Using Another Craft

This problem has not yet been solved satisfactorily. All methods more or less endanger the helper. Therefore, the safety bag together with the flotation bags are the best safeguards for a boat because they reduce reliance upon outside help.

The following method is effective: Loops that reach the cockpit rim are affixed to bow and or stern. By means of a snap-hook, they are attached near the cockpit rim in such a way that they can be released immediately. On rescuing the boat, detach the loop of the craft and throw it over your shoulder. Drag the boat into the nearest eddy. In a dangerous situation you can glide out of the loop. On the negative side, your arms, legs or head could be caught by the loops of your own boat when you capsize or the loops could interfere with paddling when the craft is towed.

A variation of this method: The snap-hook on the rope of the drifting boat is attached to its counterpart on your boat, preferably in front of the cockpit rim. The craft is then dragged by ferrying. This procedure is less cumbersome and less dangerous in the event of an upset. For blocked or familiar wild-water, where the loss of the boat would not be an unwarranted risk or the boat could be recovered around the next bend, simply push the drifting boat with the bow of your craft into the nearest eddy. Even though it does not work all the time, it is the least dangerous of the three methods.

Salvage of a Boat from Ashore

Let us suppose a friend capsized on a wild-water stretch studded with boulders. His boat drifted off. Without rescue, it will probably be lost or badly damaged. The boat should be overtaken and a suitable spot should be located to land and secure your own craft. Then, salvage the boat as you would routinely in blocked water. If the rescuing person might be endangered, secure him with a rescue line held by one or more companions.

Problems

- The drifted boat escapes again while you are securing your craft.
- Your boat is not secured properly and drifts off too.

Salvage of a Paddle

A capsize could result in a paddle floating away. Few boaters carry a spare one because paddles are too expensive.
Pick up the floating paddle and throw it to the bank. If this is not possible, use the paddle with your own like a double-decker. However, differently handed paddles cannot be used together. Don't throw your paddle onto the bank by mistake because the differently handed paddle may cause you to capsize.

To avoid losing paddles, they used to be affixed to a line. But this proved to be too risky. The paddler could be strangled or seriously hampered by the line.
On trips which would be jeopardized by the loss of paddles, attach a small stainless steel hook on the end of the shaft. When capsizing is inevitable, slip the hook onto the loop. In this way, you have one free hand which makes rescue of the boat much easier. If the snap-hook is fastened in the middle of the shaft, the paddle could act as a drag anchor, which would be detrimental.

The Rescue of a Companion in Haystacks with the Help of Your Boat

This method is necessary when prolonged swimming would endanger the life of your friend.
The companion crawls over the stern onto the deck. He lies flat, close to the cockpit, to distribute the weight more evenly.

Problems

- The companion attempts to climb aboard from one of the sides, which may upset the boat.
- The companion's legs hang over the side of the boat and impede the boat's maneuverability.

The Rescue of a Companion in Blocked Wild-Water from Ashore

In this event, follow analogously the instructions given in the section "Salvage of a Boat from Ashore."

The Rescue of a Companion by Throwing a Rope

A companion is swimming toward a dangerous spot. No time can be lost. By inspecting the white-water prior to floating, such situations can usually be foreseen. Prior to the run, find an elevated, safe position from which to throw a rope if necessary. Throw the rescue line across the river as far as possible in front of the companion. He will reach the rope, grab it, and be driven to shore by the current. By pulling, you can get him to shore faster.

Problems

- A suitable spot from which to throw a rope is not located ahead of time. The capsize occurs so suddenly and unexpectedly that unorganized attempts at rescue are ineffectual.
- The rope is not coiled twist-free before it is thrown, thus reducing the range it can be thrown.
- The rescuer throws the rope at the swimmer, instead of in front of him, and will probably miss him.

● The rope is thrown from an un-favorable spot and caught in boulders or trees.

A further example:

A capsized companion is perched upon a boulder, which he cannot safely leave. The rope is thrown in such a way that the current drifts it toward the stranded individual. The rope is thrown as far as possible. If the river downstream is dangerous, the person should rope himself around chest and shoulders by means of a butterfly noose.

Problem

● The rope is tied around the stomach, which causes shortness of breath and possible suffocation if the water pressure is high.

Another rescue method is:

A rescuer is roped. He reaches the companion and ties him to a second rope.

The Rescue of a Companion from a Dam or Roller Wave

Most fatal accidents occur at dams. The rescue line is tied to an inner tube. The inner tube is thrown as far as possible with the rope coiled twist-free. The float keeps the rope on the water surface, ready for the capsized person to grab it. Continuous jerking can prevent the rope from being sucked underwater. Pull in the rescued person laterally rather than against the current, which might offer too much resistance.

Problem

● Panic can motivate others to jump into the dangerous water near a dam, thereby risking their lives as well.

Sending a roped rescuer into the dam is highly perilous. The rope might be sucked underwater or the helpers onshore may be unable to pull the rescuer and the capsized victim free from the grip of the current.

The Rescue of a Companion from a Tree

Commonly, fatal situations result from capsizes at a fallen tree. This happens most often on flooded streams with inexperienced boaters, who cannot escape the obstruction. But even paddlers familiar with wild-water have such accidents.

In most cases, rescue within a few minutes is nearly impossible. The victim is pressed into the boat and under the tree by the current. Rescue must be swift. Climb out on the tree or to the victim from downriver and help him free himself from the boat. In

some cases, smashing the boat is necessary. Moving the tree from side-to-side or up and down can sometimes dislocate the boat from the clutch of the tree.

After rescuing the victim, artificial respiration is often called for.

Problem

● The anxious rescuer swims downstream to the accident scene, is swept into the tree, and cannot help at all. On the contrary, he too needs to be rescued.

Training for Technique

Training on Water

The choice of suitable training grounds determines on whether the wild-water beginner will progress quickly or will give up prematurely for lack of progress.

Begin in smooth water with flat banks. The water should be less than three feet deep, warm, and clean with sand or gravel on the bottom. Muddy water discourages learning the Eskimo roll. The beach is suitable for the intermediate. There a breaker, less than three feet high, can serve as practice for rollers. Have the breaker meet the boat broadside.

Equipment

This is a short list of equipment needed. More detailed information is provided in the section "Equipment."

- Maneuverable boat
- one-piece paddle
- 2 flotation bags
- wet suit pants or other types of pants to protect legs when tipping over
- life jacket and wet suit tunic if water is cold.
- sprayskirt
- tennis shoes or neoprene boots
- bathing suit and towel
- suntan lotion
- sunglasses
- first-aid kit (with tweezers to remove fiberglass slivers)
- sponge, tied to the boat

To practice technique, set up a course of at least 20 gates by means of poles or anchored buoys. For slalom, at least 40. Be certain to secure glasses and to take off your watch if it isn't waterproof.

Time required

Only information on the average time required can be given. Progress depends on many factors, such as, physical fitness, equipment, trainer or companions, training grounds, and weather.

At least 3 days must be calculated for the beginner to learn the basic form of all techniques. Advanced paddlers also require 3 days to practice all techniques, including slalom and the Eskimo roll. On the whole, you will notice that the basic skill can be acquired in a comparatively short period of time if the student practices 5 to 6 hours per day.

Paddling without a Boat

The target of this training is to develop the capability and quick reaction time to the forces arising from the paddle meeting water. The more you experiment, the better. Without a boat, you do not have to worry about balance. You feel directly the forces resulting from the paddle moving through the water.

The wild-water boater handles the paddle in the following manner. First find out whether you have a right- or left-handed paddle. The paddle is held horizontally in such a way that the concave side (see section "Equipment") of one blade faces upward while the other curves toward the boater. If the concave side of the right blade faces the paddler, his right hand is fixed, that is, it keeps a constant grip on the shaft. Here is the way to do it: grasp the shaft in such a way that the back of the right hand forms a 90-degree angle to the right blade. Never alter this grip. Your left hand is unfixed, that is, it maintains a loose grip to allow the shaft to turn freely within it. If the concave side of the left blade faces the paddler, the left hand will accordingly be the fixed one.

For proper spacing of your hands, grasp the paddle in such a way that your elbows are bent at 90-degree angles when holding the shaft in the horizontal position above your head.

Physics

According to the principle, action equals reaction, the movement (action) of the blade through the water generates corresponding forces (reaction) which differ according to the angle between the blade and direction of the movement.
An object met or moved by a liquid will always drift towards lee.

Exercises

- Paddle forward in shallow water with the rotating fist bent upward when you pull the other blade through the water.
- Paddle backward the same way.
- Pull paddle from bow to stern with the shaft held almost horizontally so that the blade generates a dynamic buoyancy.
- Pull paddle alternately toward bow and stern with the shaft held almost horizontally and the concave side of the blade facing downward, so that a dynamic buoyancy arises.
- Deliberate slicing down and turning up again of the blade.

All these exercises and their combinations should be practiced until there in no longer any uncertainty or tendency to reverse the blades. In wildwater, you will have no time to check

whether the blade is inserted into the water at the correct angle.

Mistakes

- The paddle is grasped disproportionately or asymmetrically.
- The spacing between the two fists is too narrow.
- The thumb does not enclose the shaft.
- The shaft rotates in both hands.
- The grip on the shaft is altered.
- The concave side of the blade faces the bow when it is pulled through the water.

The static paddle brace, that is, the flat handling and bracing on the blade, is not described because it leads to a passive and inflexible behavior on the part of the beginner which later on frequently results in capsizing.
Remember that the paddle is not a flotation bag. Either the paddle or the water or both are moved. This is called the dynamic paddle brace.

Embarking, Sitting, Disembarking

The narrow cockpit of the modern wild-water boat requires a special technique in embarking and disembarking. In addition, the paddler must get in the proper position in relation to seat, foot brace, knee and hip braces which transmits the power to the boat. After a little practice, boats that require the proverbial shoehorn are no longer frightening.

Technique

- Sit in the boat and adjust the foot brace ashore.
- Launch the boat.
- Squat beside the cockpit.
- Rest one blade of the paddle behind the cockpit rim with the other blade lying flat on shore.
- Grasp shaft (or blade) and cockpit rim in one hand and support your weight by the outer arm on the bridged paddle.
- Sit on the cockpit rim and shift your legs one at a time into the boat.

Reverse the procedure for disembarking.

Control

Correct sitting position keeps your

Embarking with bridged paddle: squat, sit on the cockpit rim, swing legs into the boat.

1

2

3

4

torso leaning forward slightly without effort. The balls of your feet rest on the brace. The knees or upper thighs touch the deck (knee braces, cockpit molds, knee molds) without wasting energy. When leaning backward, your head touches the quarter-deck without interference from the rear cockpit rim (see section "Eskimo Roll"). Between seat and hip braces, free play should be very small. Otherwise, foot and hip bracing is ineffectual. On the river, the bridged paddle guarantees the safest embarking. In shallow water and even between two boats it is the best way to get into the boat. It guards against the current taking control of the boat at the moment of embarking.

Physics

On entering or exiting a kayak, the wild-water boater's high center of gravity could easily capsize the craft. By distributing the body weight between boat and shore, a stable equilibrium is established.

Mistakes

- Your feet do not reach the foot brace. Adjust it!
- The foot brace is too tight. The legs cannot be straddled underneath the deck. Adjust it!
- The seat is too broad. Attach foam rubber to the sides.

- The back rubs against the seat. Install foam rubber. You could remove the rear part of the seat.

Fastening the Sprayskirt

The sprayskirt protects the space between paddler and cockpit rim against penetrating water. Particularly on wild-water cruising where the boat often submerges completely, it is indispensable and should fit perfectly. Prior to embarking, step into the sprayskirt and tie the drawstring around the waist. When sitting in the boat, fit the sprayskirt around the cockpit rim by means of the shock cord sewn into the bottom of the sprayskirt.

To remove the sprayskirt, pull the shock cord attachment free from the cockpit rim. In an emergency, the sprayskirt should automatically detach from the boat when you exit the boat. The sprayskirt should not snap off the cockpit rim if you lean forward or backward, bend to the side, or bang heavily on the sprayskirt with your hand. However, it should come off if you exit with force.

Mistake

- Tape the sprayskirt to the boat to make it more resistant to water

Lean forward and backward to check free-dom of movement. A wild-water craft should not interfere with movements of the torso.

pressure. A very dangerous practice!

Capsizing and the Wet Exit

Many beginners are unreasonably afraid of capsizing. They cannot imagine how they can escape the narrow cockpit underwater. Therefore, practice the technique of underwater exiting and familiarize yourself with it from the very beginning. Practice first without a sprayskirt.

Technique in a Kayak

- First put your legs together so that you can turn your body as a unit to the side, bend simultaneously at the waist, and lean your torso forward. Thus, you head remains near the water surface and is protected by the angled arm.

- Push off from the foot brace and remove the sprayskirt if you have not already done so.

Physics

The buoyancy (life vest) which affects the torso of the capsized paddler acts upon the boat like a torque which is no longer transferred when the legs are put together. Thus, the paddler can leave the cockpit and boat, if necessary by using his hands and feet.

Exercises

- After the trainee capsizes, the trainer takes the hand of the trainee and submerges with him. This reduces the beginner's fear and helps him to exit the boat.

- The trainee capsizes alone but stays underwater as long as possible. He relaxes underwater and

improves his orientation by bending the torso to the left and the right, forward and backward. When he runs out of breath, he exits the boat.

Remember

- Put legs together.
- Bend at the waist and lean forward.
- Hold onto the paddle.
- Grab the loop of the boat.

Mistakes

- The paddler leans backward and is caught on the cockpit rim. The life vest presses him against the deck underwater. His face is unprotected when he brushes the river bottom.

- The paddler closes his eyes and cannot orient himself.

This wild-water paddler swings his boat into the tongue of the current using draw strokes supported by foot and hip bracing. The violent forces that affect a wild-water boat could cause a capsize if not counter-balanced.

● The paddler practices alone. (Never practice alone!)

The paddler may use a nose clip or snorkeling face mask. Before beginning, check for fiberglass slivers around the cockpit rim.

Emptying the Boat

Fiberglass boats and foldboats are heavier than water. Completely swamped, they will sink. This is prevented by fitting flotation bags into the boat. When running wild-water, the flotation bags not only maintain buoyancy but also prevent as much water as possible from swamping the overturned boat. Each additional cubic foot of air in the boat reduces the danger of breakage. A boat only half swamped can easily weigh 300 pounds (150 kg). Broadsiding an obstacle with this amount of weight can easily cause breakage. The foot braces, back belts, or similar equipment secures the flotation bags inside the boat. (For further measures, see section "Equipment".)

Technique

● After exiting, keep the boat up-turned.
● Drag the boat into shallow water.
● Roll it on its side and empty it of as much water as possible.

● To remove the rest of the water, put the boat over a knee and move the ends up and down. Or pull the boat up a slope and lift the lower end. The easiest way to empty a boat is with a companion.

Remember that if a fiberglass boat creaks when emptied, it is starting to break. To sponge a boat, put it on edge to concentrate the water in one spot.

The huge space of the interior of a wild-water double canoe (roughly estimated to be 25 cubic feet) holds a correspondingly high quantity of water. At times, considerable effort is required to empty it, perhaps more than a team can handle. However, a hole bored through the upper part of the hull close to the stern facilitates the emptying process. It should be small, not more than an inch in diameter. Use a plastic stopper to close the hole when floating.

Foot and Hip Bracing

A wild-water boat is designed primarily for horizontal trim with a waterline symmetrical to the longitudinal axis. In this position, it will reach maximum speed and run the easiest. By leaning the boat on its side, the waterline becomes asymmetrical and the boat turns around. At the same time, the water-line length shortens and the pivoting capacity increases. These changes in trim are achieved by foot and hip bracing.

The radius of action of the paddle can be enlarged by leaning boat and torso. The necessary stability is brought about by paddle bracing on the one hand and by foot and hip bracing on the other.

In wild-water, there are forces which would capsize a boat unless countermeasures are taken. First of all, the tongues of currents and eddies generate forces which bounce against the craft. Secondly, there are complex currents, breakers, and rollers that affect the boat. And thirdly, the centrifugal force in narrow bends influence the boat. Quick reaction with foot, leg, and hip bracing can prevent an upset. You can lean the boat in such a way that the water flows easily underneath and around the bottom. The boat that is on the verge of capsizing can be brought under the paddler's center of gravity by swinging the hips.

A boat can be trimmed to the extent that any kind of paddle bracing is unnecessary. The paddle is, however, ready to brace. Highly skillful foot and hip bracing permit the paddler to maintain his boat's trim despite water forces so that he can use the paddle strokes exclusively for maneuvering. The supporting effect of paddle bracing helps to replace the boat under the paddler's center of gravity if it is haphazardly or unexpectedly tipped. This applies particularly to the Eskimo roll. Without perfect swiveling of the hips, the Eskimo roll can be accomplished only with utmost energy consumption and at the risk of breaking the paddle.

Technique: Basic Form

- Hips, upper legs, knees, and feet counteract the forces which cause the boat to capsize.
- In the same manner, the boat is leaned and released.
- By foot and hip bracing the boat is maintained in such a position that a state of equilibrium is reached. This may require bending forward at the waist. Thus little or no reverse weight is transferred to the paddle.

Technique: Advanced Form

- Eskimo roll of a capsized boat under most difficult conditions.

Physics

Foot and hip bracing is based on the law: action equals reaction. The body's moment of inertia makes it possible to lean the boat instantane-

ously from normal trim or to release it to normal trim from the leaned position. In the extreme, the boat is rolled. The body's moment of inertia so strongly resists a sudden rotation around the boat's long axis that almost all tipping forces affecting the boat for a short period of time can be counterbalanced.

Exercises

- The trainer simulates the forces which affect the boat in wild-water.
- Demonstration of wrong counterbalancing. For example, the trainee leans away from the affecting force, bends at the waist, and capsizes because the water does not offer firm resistance to the tipping force.

- Demonstration of the correct foot and hip bracing. A trainee tries to overturn the trainer by pushing down on the left side of the trainer's boat. He counteracts by foot and hip bracing.
- The trainee is instructed to capsize by a sudden rotation of the boat around its long axis.
- The trainee is instructed to capsize by laterally rocking the boat.

Perform these exercises in both the forward and backward direction. If a trainer is unavailable, use the following method: release most of the air from the bow and stern flotation bags. With each exercise, swamp the boat a little more. Then fasten the sprayskirt and practice. For safety, stay

3

close to shore. The water slushing around in the boat can cause considerable difficulties for the novice. Once you master the exercises, capsizing will be a maneuver rather than a fearful experience.

Mistakes

- Balancing is leaning the torso away from the affecting force and bending at the waist, as cyclists and tightropers do. Yet this turns the boat in the direction of the affecting force and causes capsizing.
- The paddler does not have the right fit with the boat (see section "Embarking, Sitting, Disembarking").

To improve the sense of equilibrium, the following exercises are recommended:

- Lean the boat as far and as long as possible in shallow water. Prevent upset by paddle bracing. If necessary, support yourself with the paddle on the ground.
- Tip deliberately and prevent capsizing by paddle, foot, and hip bracing.
- Run stretches as long as possible with the boat leaned forward, paddling on both sides.

Paddling Forward in the Kayak

Even though you do not intend to participate in competitions, strive for a good paddling technique. Other-

wise, you will tire quickly and be unable to utilize the special advantages of the modern wild-water craft. Forward paddling is the right way to propel the boat straight ahead, to accelerate it, to move it through wide curves, out of roller waves and turbulent stretches, to cross currents and stabilize the trim.

After practicing foot and hip bracing, the beginner can now concentrate on correctly executed strokes. Expect to have difficulty with keeping the boat going on a straight course. Practice will give the boater the feel for slightest deviations and he will learn to align his craft almost unconsciously.

Forward paddling in the kayak: lean forward, stretch back arm, insert the paddle into the water smoothly.

2

1

Technique: Basic Form

See "Paddling without a Boat" for information about right- and left-handed paddles as well as how to hold the paddle.

- The blade should be moved through the water parallel to the boat's long axis.
- From inserting to slicing out, the blade keeps a 90-degree angle to the boat's long axis.

Technique: Advanced Form

- The paddle stroke is made close to the hull.
- The blade is inserted as far forward as is comfortable without splashing and then accelerated.
- The torso leans forward.
- The forward arm is stretched when the blade is inserted.
- The paddle is pulled through the water just up to the paddler's waist.
- The backward hand starts moving at eye level.
- The blade is brought out of the water without a splash near the hips.
- Do not move the backward hand further than the middle of the boat.
- The feet should touch the foot brace rhythmically (draw right; press left) to maintain the circulation of blood in the legs.
- The shoulders are likewise turned.
- Right-handers rotate the shaft with the right hand; left-handers with the left one.

Physics

The blade of the paddle is more resistant in the water than the boat is. As a consequence, the force affecting the paddle moves the boat through the water. The kayak is not propelled simulataneously from both sides like a rowboat is. Thus, the kayak deviates from alignment. But by pulling the blade of the paddle parallel and as close as possible to the boat's long axis, maximum efficiency from the stroke is achieved. The farther from the hull the paddle is in the water and the more the stroke resembles an arc, the greater is the boat's deviation from a straight course. The bow rises slightly with each paddle stroke because the paddle is not inserted into the water vertically. This in turn increases the boat's resistance. Maximum propulsion results from a blade inserted at a 90-degree angle to the paddling direction with the concave side facing the stern.

Advantages

The low susceptibility of the blade to lateral currents or lateral displacement makes it possible to master even unclear current differentials by foot and hip bracing.

Disadvantages

The advanced technique, particularly in racing, requires steep handling of the shaft which can cause capsizing. The following exercises teach the paddler to alternate steep and flat handling of the shaft.

Exercises

- Slowly paddle the boat forward. Do not back paddle to counterbalance deviations from a straight course. Increase speed only gradually.
- Paddle toward a target 100 yards away without correcting the course.
- Paddle toward a target increasing speed intermittently.
- Alternate between steep and flat handling of the shaft to increase the bracing effect.
- Lean the boat slightly by hip bracing and paddle forward symmetrically (the boat should turn).
- Lean the boat and paddle on one side (the boat turns sharply).
- Maneuver the boat on a slalom course through pairs of poles or buoys.

Remember

- Lean forward.
- Extend the arms when the paddle is moving from the horizontal position.
- Insert the blade smoothly.

Mistakes

- Paddling along the gunwale.
- The blade is moved in an arc instead of along a straight line.
- Bouncing the paddle on the water.
- The back arm does not push forward. It remains bent and the paddling power must be exerted by the forward arm.
- The paddle is pulled through the water beyond the hips of the boater.

Paddle Bracing

To reduce the risk of capsizing, transfer little weight to the paddle when bracing. Propel the boat with very short strokes. If necessary, paddle with flat shaft and flatly inserted blade.

Tape the shaft of the paddle where you grip it. This provides good handling qualities because your hands won't slip. In addition, it locates the correct distance between the hands and achieves symmetry.

Slowing Down, Paddling Backward

The ability to back paddle and slow down is important. Before the draw stroke was borrowed from canoeing by kayakers, lateral displacement of the kayak was achieved by ferrying, that is, by back paddling. Even though it is not a sensational technique, ferrying enables a kayaker to master an extremely difficult wild-water stretch when nothing else works. Ferrying will be described in more detail in the section "Training in Haystacks." Ferrying is a basic technique in rafting with big inflated boats to avoid obstructions.

Technique: Basic Form

- Slowing down: About at hip level, the paddle blade is inserted into the water vertically. Alternate the blade to the left and right side to cancel out some of the boat's motion. Back paddle slowly.
- Paddling backward: Insert the paddle to the left and right side alternately behind the hip. Push forward with the blade.

Technique: Advanced Form

Slowing down and paddling backward:

- Paddle with very short strokes.

- Paddle as close to the hull as possible.
- Push forward parallel to the boat's long axis.

Each braking stroke causes a change of alignment. Counterbalance the stroke by turning the outer blade edge backward. In this position slice the blade backward and outward. Pull it finally toward the stern without changing the blade angle. Then make the next brake or back stroke.

Physics

The forward movement of the boat must be counteracted by resistance on both sides. The unavoidable deviations from alignment are kept as small as possible by short strokes spaced close to the boat.

Exercises

- Slow down from high speed without turning the craft.
- Back paddle toward a target from a distance of at least 100 yards with the head turned of course in the cruising direction.

Mistakes

- By concentrating on slowing down you maneuver on one side. The boat turns athwart.
- Back leaning too much. The boat broaches.

- The concave side of the blade faces the bow. With the following forward stroke, the risk of capsize is great.
- A flat handling of the shaft makes the boat turn too sharply with each back stroke.

To paddle brace when slowing down or back paddling, insert the blade in such a way that it generates a dynamic buoyancy. The angle depends on the direction and velocity of the current. Flatter insertion increases the bracing effect.

Rhythm of paddling in the C 2: lean forward and insert the blade steeply; while pulling the paddle blade, sit upright again; lean forward and insert blade steeply.

Paddling Forward in the Canoe

The kayaker's forward stroke cannot be applied to canoeing, despite equivalent physical fundamentals. Because of the forward lean of the boater's torso when inserting the paddle in the water, the canoe is more jerky on acceleration and at maximum speed than the kayak, which moves smoothly and uniformly. In addition, a steering stroke is necessary for straight running in a canoe. Otherwise, the boater must continuously move the paddle from one side to the other.

The single paddle is always turned with the palm of the upper hand over the top of the grip. The other hand guides or supports the turn of the paddle.

Technique: Basic Form

When a canoe paddle is held properly, a somewhat smaller than 90-degree angle exists between upper arm and forearm.

- Lean forward to insert the paddle into the water. Straighten the torso to an upright position when the paddle is pulled through the water.
- Hold the shaft vertically when inserting the blade and pulling it through the water.
- Pull the paddle through the water parallel to the keel, that is, in the cruising direction.

4

3

● Steering stroke: The stern man turns the outer edge of the blade backwards, prior to removing the blade from the water.

Technique: Advanced Form

● Insert the blade a short distance from the bow and turn the outer edge of the blade backward. When you start pulling, the bow is dragged aside, thus balancing the one-sided propulsion. This is especially important when accelerating the canoe from zero.

● Insert the blade smoothly and accelerate during the pull.

● In slalom competition, the paddle blade is sliced forward along the gunwale and thus used for steer-ing if the arrangement of a gate makes this necessary.

● In shallow water, flat handling of the shaft can prevent the paddle from being knocked out of the paddler's hands.

Exercises

● The same recommendations hold true for practicing both the canoe-ing and kayaking techniques.

● Beginners should start as the bow man to free them from the burden of the steering stroke.

● Paddle bracing during the forward pull of the paddle should be prac-ticed with particular intensity.

● Cooperation between the paddlers is important. Positions should be changed frequently to familiarize both boaters with the reactions of the canoe.

● In slalom competition, steering is no longer exclusively executed by the stern man. The bow man has the better vantage on wild-water.

He starts the maneuvers neces-sary to evade obstructions and the stern man prevents the boat from broaching.

● The canoeing technique is best developed by means of a slalom course.

● To lower the center of gravity and to make the boat more resistant to upset, the canoe team leans simultaneously to the side of pad-dle bracing. This technique must be practiced intensively.

2   1

Mistakes

- The blade is not completely inserted into the water.
- The shaft is too long.
- The steering stroke is too hasty.
- The paddle is not grasped with the palm of the upper hand over the top of the grip.
- The bow man paddles along the gunwale instead of in keel direction. Thus the craft turns continuously.

To paddle brace, lean towards the paddle and paddle forward to achieve a lower center of gravity and to increase stability. Begin the paddle brace after completing the forward stroke and removing the paddle from the water.

Sweep in Kayak and Canoe

The sweep is one of the simplest and most reliable techniques. Whether the craft is moving or not, the sweep can turn it into a new direction or turn it around completely. It can be used to evade obstructions or to swing from a tongue of the current into an eddy. Because of its simplicity, the sweep is sometimes applied carelessly and wastefully by paddlers.

Technique: Basic Form

- Insert the blade flatly and make an arc, beginning close to the bow and ending close to the stern.

Technique: Advanced Form

- The forward arm remains stretched during the entire stroke. The backward arm is bent.
- Slight change of the 90-degree blade angle generates some buoyancy.
- Lean forward to increase the reach of the paddle.
- Insert the blade without splashing and accelerate it.
- At the end of the stroke when the paddle is brought out of the water, slide it forward as a paddle brace.
- Leaning sideways during the sweep increases maneuverability.
- In a canoe, extend the forward arm for the sweep by modifying the spacing.
- A sweep in the bow and a back sweep in the stern, or vice versa, turns the canoe around.

Physics

The paddle stroke pushes the bow aside because water offers more resistance to the movement of the blade than to a turn of the boat on its pivot point.

On straight forward paddling, the boat is in an unstable equilibrium around its pivot point. To disturb this state of equilibrium by a stroke, or the current, the center of gravity tries to continue its straight ahead movement. A light force is sufficient to turn the boat on its pivot point.

Advantages

The sweep, especially at slow speeds, turns the boat and accelerates it simultaneously. This is an important manuever to evade obstructions on wild-water. Unlike the back sweep, the sweep does not push the stern towards the obstacle and the boat can be brought more quickly from the current into an eddy for a landing.

Disadvantage

When the boat is traveling at high speeds, an extreme sweep can cause a capsize.

Exercises

- Turn the boat in normal trim by 360 degrees using the sweep.
- Turn the boat by 360 degrees using as few sweeps as possible, pay attention to acceleration during the sweep.
- Turn the boat while leaning outward and bracing simultaneously.
- Accelerate the boat and turn it

from its straight course by a sweep.

- For wild-water cruising, the following stroke is important: Pass from a normal forward stroke to a sweep by flattening the shaft and stretching the forward arm.
- Slalom paddling with sweep and forward strokes.

Mistakes

- The forward arm is angled.
- The paddle is inserted too hastily and without acceleration.
- The boat's velocity is too high.
- The concave side of the blade faces the boat at the beginning.
- Sufficient foot and hip bracing is necessary when the sweep ends at the stern and the paddler is leaning outward. Otherwise, capsizing results.

The sweep performed with a flat shaft generates such buoyancy that, together with the movement of the hips, even the Eskimo roll is possible.

Back Sweep

The back sweep is a reflex action when you see an obstacle ahead. However, it embarrasses the wild-water beginner more often than it assists him. Combined with other strokes and rightly applied, the back sweep is an important maneuvering aid to the wild-water paddler. It can turn the boat and swing it either in or out of the current.

Technique: Basic Form

- The paddle is pushed forward in slicing out position. In this way, it corresponds to a back stroke.
- The forward arm remains angled as does the backward arm.

Technique: Advanced Form

- Stationary boat:
  Hold the shaft as flat as possible. Hold the paddle as if you just completed a forward stroke. Push it outward, beginning close to the stern and continuing through an arc.
- Moving boat:
  A steering stroke initiates the turn (see "Paddling Forward in a Canoe"). The back sweep follows. By leaning into the turn, maneuverability is increased. After initiating the turn, the paddle is released by foot and hip bracing to such an extent that it slides across the water just for security reasons.
- Canoe:
  A back sweep of the bow man and a sweep by the stern man, or vice versa, turns the boat.

Physics

The same laws hold true as described in connection with the sweep. It is important to shorten the waterline in order to increase maneuverability. On the other hand, leaning the boat into the turn makes the water pass underneath the stern easier.

Disadvantages

On evasive maneuvers, the stern is pushed toward the obstruction. Because the back sweep is nearly a reflex action, it can turn into panicky reactions under pressure, especially with an inexperienced boater.

Exercises

- Turn the boat with normal trim by 360 degrees with back sweeps.
- Turn the boat by 360 degrees with as few back sweeps as possible. Pay attention to the acceleration during back sweep.
- Turn the boat while leaning outward and simultaneously bracing.
- Accelerate the boat and swing it by a back sweep combined with bracing.
- Combine sweep and back sweep as a means of evasion.

Remember

- Push paddle away from stern.
- Accelerate stroke.

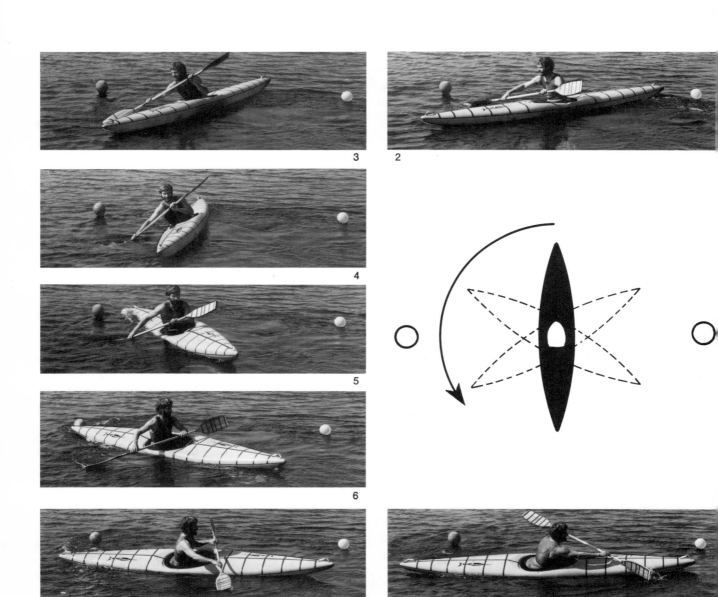

1

14

13

12

11

The sweep is one of the simplest and
most reliable paddling techniques. You
can turn the boat without speed to evade
obstructions or to swing up into an eddy.

9

10

1

2

3

4

5

6

Swinging up. Guide swinging up with a sweep while leaning the boat. Follow with a back sweep brace.

- Brace smooth or just secure during the turn.
- Lean the boat slightly into the turn.

Mistakes

- The paddle is hastily pushed downward instead of away from the boat.
- Too much weight is suspended on the blade because foot and hip bracing is still underdeveloped. Due to the braking effect of the blade, the boat turns less.

Extension of the forward arm causes more effective bracing. However, attention must be paid to a sufficiently high difference in speed between blade and water.

Draw Technique or "Canoe Stroke"

Inspired by canoeing, the use of different draw strokes in the kayak extends the range of navigable waters for the wild-water expert. This is especially true if ferry gliding cannot be applied or if the time element in downriver racing or slalom competition prohibits the use of ferry gliding. Fiberglass boats with their smooth surface are perfectly suited for the draw technique, which, like ferry gliding, is found in rafting, the oldest type of wild-water cruising.

From innumerable variations and combinations with other strokes, the following is a discussion of the most interesting ones for wild-water. However, practice usually involves maximum difficulties if the techniques described so far are not mastered perfectly. It is indispensable to study theory and practice of the draw technique as thoroughly as possible to make use of its manifold advantages in wild-water paddling. Otherwise, unnecessary energy expenditure, puzzling reactions of the boat, and surprising capsizes can overwhelm the boater. The simple draw stroke is applied to evade obstacles, achieve lateral displacement, cross rapid tongues of currents, swing and run cross-breakers and cross-rollers.

Technique: Basic Form

- Without speed, the boat can be displaced laterally by inserting the blade perpendicularly abeam of the paddler and parallel to cruising direction. Pull the blade towards the boat. The inner edge of the blade is simultaneously turned forward. But the grip at the shaft is not altered. The concave side of the blade faces the boat.
- Just before reaching the gunwale, the front edge of the blade is turned towards the boat again.

- Hold the paddle shaft as vertically as possible.
- Insert the entire blade into the water.
- A draw stroke on the off-side of the rotating hand should be executed with the wrist strongly bent backward for correct blade angle.

Technique: Advanced Form

Constant lateral displacement of the moving or motionless boat is achieved by a series of draw strokes one after the other.

- Insert the blade into the water and pull it toward the boat. Slice the blade outward in the water and pull again toward the boat. Repeat this as often as is necessary to attain the correct boat position.
- Extend the radius of action by leaning the boat toward the paddle at the beginning of the draw stroke. At the end of the stroke, return to the upright position.
- To move a fast-running boat laterally and to accelerate at the same time: The draw stroke becomes a forward stroke by returning the front edge of the blade toward the boat.
- The canoe is turned by simultaneous draw strokes in bow and stern.

Physics

By pulling the blade of the paddle toward the boat, two power components effect the craft. One displaces the boat laterally and the other generates a dynamic buoyancy. The buoyancy is increased by inserting a flat blade and by quickly pulling the paddle toward the boat. The power of the pull increases with the more horizontal the shaft is held and the longer the blade path is in the water. As with other paddle strokes, the bracing effect increases with the extension of the forward arm.

Advantages

The draw stroke is important for wild-water maneuvering. On evading an obstacle, the boat does not swerve from alignment as is the case with the sweep and the back sweep. In the event of a collision, the capsizing risk is considerably reduced. The draw stroke achieves lateral displacement more quickly than does ferry gliding or a combination of sweep and back sweep. The simultaneous bracing effect of the draw technique improves safe cruising.

Disadvantages

The many advantages are partly counterbalanced by the possibility in shallow water that the paddle could be lost, damaged, or broken. Fur-

The sweep turns the slow moving boat and accelerates it at the same time. This is important in escaping from obstacles in wild-water. Unlike the back sweep, the sweep does not push the stern towards the obstruction. In the canoe, the turn is achieved by a combination of strokes. Pictures 1–14 show a turn by the bowman using a sweep and the sternman using a back sweep.

5   4   3

thermore, the boat could be thrown across the vertically inserted paddle in very high irregular waves or turbulent current.

Compared to the Duffek stroke, the most widespread variant of the draw technique, the draw stroke has less bracing effect.

Exercises

The draw position of the paddle, which seems rather difficult at first, can be learned quickly by the following exercises:

● Hold the paddle horizontally, which is the basic position of the forward stroke. Lift the forward hand until

the forearm is vertical and the upper arm is horizontal. This puts the shaft vertical to the water surface.

● The forearm of the forward hand is then turned outward so it forms a 90-degree angle with the boat's long axis and the blade is parallel to it. This is the draw position.

1   2   3

2   1

- Practice basic and draw positions alternately until you are familiar with them and can do them without changing the grip.

- Practice the draw stroke alternately at the right and left side.

- For further exercises, see "Technique: Basic Form" and "Advanced Form."

Mistakes

- The shaft is twisted in the rotating hand which creates a high capsize risk with the following forward stroke.

Swinging up with a back sweep. Push paddle away from the stern. Brace easily. Lean boat into the turn.

Lateral displacement of the boat. Bend back arm around your head. Insert the blade completely into the water. Draw the blade toward the boat. Lean toward the paddle. Slice paddle outward.

4

5

6

- The shaft is too horizontal which results in much dynamic buoyancy but little displacing pull.
- The draw stroke is initiated too close to the stern behind the hip. Even though this stroke takes a great deal of energy and strength, it turns the stern rather than the bow.
- The draw stroke is performed too hastily, usually with the blade not inserted deep enough.
- Too little foot and hip bracing while leaning in the direction of the draw stroke can cause an upset.

The bracing effect can be increased by flattening the shaft to a horizontal position, by vigorously pulling the blade, and by utilizing the current.

To change from normal position to draw or Duffek position. Note the concave side of the blade facing the bow.

Duffek Stroke

The Duffek stroke, named after a Czech slalom specialist, is the most frequently observed variant of the draw technique. It achieves quick, precise maneuvering, such as, an eddy turn or swinging into the tongue of a current. This holds true for wild-water cruising but even more for slalom competition which would be unimaginable without this stroke.

Technique: Basic Form

Traveling with speed, the boater inserts the blade of the paddle perpendicularly abeam of his knee in such a way that it forms a 45-degree angle with the bow. The concave side of the blade, which usually faces the stern, now faces the bow. Thus, the boat is turned around. This is the steering phase.

Technique: Advanced Form

In the advanced form a distinction can be made between steering, draw, and propelling phases.

- After inserting the blade into the water, the paddler waits until the draw at the blade relaxes (steering phase).
- Then, the blade is turned parallel to cruising direction and drawn towards the boat (draw phase).
- The blade is turned again. The concave side faces the stern once again and forms the propelling phase.
- The radius of action of the paddle can be extended by leaning the boat toward the blade during the steering and draw phases and returning to the upright position at the end of the draw phase.

The boat's reaction to the Duffek

Steering phase of the Duffek stroke. Insert the blade at knee level and turn the concave side of the blade toward the bow at a 45-degree angle. This turns the boat.

stroke depends on the direction in which the craft is moving at the time the stroke is applied.

- If the boat is moving straight ahead, it is slightly displaced laterally into a narrow turn.
- If turning toward the direction of the stroke, the turn is intensified, quickly becoming a 90-degree swing.
- If turning away from the direction of the stroke, a mere parallel displacement may result.

Physics

When the blade turns 45 degrees with the concave side facing the bow, two power components affect it. One displaces the boat laterally and the other generates a dynamic buoyancy. These two forces result in a braking power at the paddle, acting as a pivot point around which the boat skids. This happens if the boat is moving forward at normal speed.

As soon as the bow is lifted by speed or by counter-, cross-, or slower currents, the boat's pivot point shifts behind its center of gravity, offering high resistance to any turn. Then, a Duffek stroke draws the boat aside. The turn begins later and is minimal. Further details are given under "Technique: Advanced Form." As is the case with the draw stroke, efficiency increases

with a more vertical shaft hold and the better the blade angle is adjusted to the specific situation.

Advantages

Compared to the draw stroke, the long steering phase increases the dynamic stability as a consequence of its buoyancy (bracing effect).

Exercises

- Hold the paddles horizontally in standard position. Lift the forward hand until the forearm is vertical and the upper arm is horizontal. Then, the shaft is also in a vertical position.
- The forearm of the forward hand is then turned outward until it forms a 90-degree angle to the boat's long axis and the blade is parallel to it. This is the draw position.
- To reach the Duffek position, the upper controlling hand must be bent backward until the blade forms a 45-degree angle to the boat's long axis (steering phase).
- If necessary the rotating hand must be slightly turned too in order to obtain a forward facing blade.
- Practice standard and Duffek positions alternately until the change is completely mastered. Of particular importance is the change at the

off-side of the rotating hand – that is, in the case of a right-handed paddle, practice the Duffek stroke at the left side. Otherwise, so-called "strong sides" are favored.

- These exercises should be completely mastered in smooth water before attempting them during a trip.
- The Duffek stroke with following draw and forward strokes should be practiced until they can be executed over a distance of several hundred yards alternately at the right and left sides without loss of speed. This teaches you the correct way to handle the shaft.

Remember

- Put backward arm around your head.
- Turn blade so that the concave side faces the bow.
- Keep blade in the water long enough.

Control

- By means of a Duffek stroke, a kayak can be turned quickly by 90 degrees and displaced laterally by at least 3 yards.

Mistakes

- The shaft is twisted in the rotating hand. As a consequence, the

blade gravitates in the following forward stroke.

- The boat is moving in the wrong direction when the Duffek stroke begins. For example, it moves toward the left when it is to be swung into an eddy at the right side. This results in an undesired parallel displacement.

The bracing effect is increased by horizontal handling of the shaft, high speed, and a pronounced turning of the blade.

Sculling

Sculling differs from a continuous series of draw strokes in that it displaces the boat laterally without jerks. It is applicable when the boat runs at slow speed or is stationary. The canoe is turned around by simultaneous sculling at bow and stern.

Technique: Basic Form

- Hold the shaft as vertical as possible.
- The concave side of the blade faces the bow at a 45-degree angle. Draw the blade toward the bow and turn it by 90 degrees so the concave side now faces the stern. Pull backward. The procedure can be repeated as often as

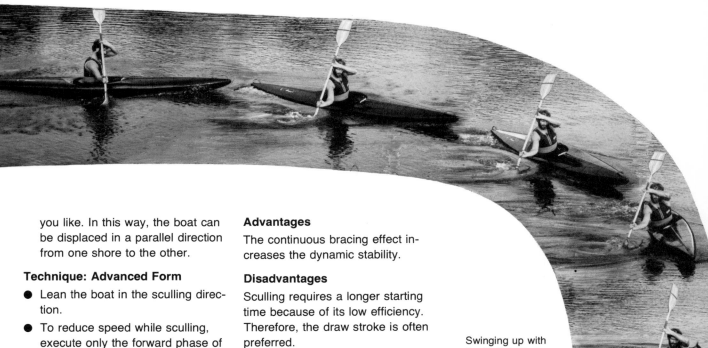

you like. In this way, the boat can be displaced in a parallel direction from one shore to the other.

Technique: Advanced Form

- Lean the boat in the sculling direction.
- To reduce speed while sculling, execute only the forward phase of the stroke and then slice the blade backward. To accelerate, do the reverse.

Physics

Two power components affect the blade moving through the water at a 45-degree angle. One draws the blade away from the boat. The other moves the boat alternately forward and backward. These movements partly counterbalance each other producing a bracing effect.

Advantages

The continuous bracing effect increases the dynamic stability.

Disadvantages

Sculling requires a longer starting time because of its low efficiency. Therefore, the draw stroke is often preferred.

Exercises

Sculling is learned rather easily through the following exercises. The buoyancy generated at the blade is transformed into a lateral draw by holding the shaft more and more vertically.

- Alternate continuously between sweep and back sweep with flattened blade.
- Raise the backward arm gradually

Swinging up with the Duffek stroke. Put back arm around your head. Insert blade vertically and turn the concave side toward the bow. Leave blade in the water.

1

2

3

and finally put it over your head. This makes the boat move laterally.

- Practice the alteration between vertical and horizontal handling of the shaft in order to increase the dynamic stability.

Remember

- Put backward arm over the head.
- Hold the concave side of the blade slantwise facing the cruising direction.

Mistakes

- Moving the paddle too fast re-

duces the efficiency of the stroke.

- Horizontal handling of the shaft and a strongly angled blade increase dynamic stability but causes little lateral displacement.

Repeated Prystroke

The repeated pry is the counterpart of the sculling stroke. Particularly suited for canoes and smaller inflated boats, the pry displaces the boat lat-

erally, turns, and swings it. With narrower boats, the repeated pry usually involves too many risks because it lacks the bracing effect found with other paddle strokes. The usable supporting power of the stroke is of no interest to the standard wild-water paddler.

Technique: Basic Form

- The inner edge of the blade is turned athwart toward the bow and the paddle is pushed forward along the gunwale.
- There, the paddle is turned 90 degrees with the inner edge pointing

4

5

6

Lateral displacement by sculling. Wrap back arm around your head. The concave side of the blade faces the cruising direction crosswise.

backward and athwart and is pulled backward along the gunwale.

Technique: Advanced Form
- Insert the shaft vertically into the water.
- Generally a 45-degree blade angle has the highest efficiency. It must, however, be adjusted to the movements of the boat, the actions of the partner, and the current.
- If the speed is to be reduced simultaneously, only the forward phase of the repeated pry is performed and the blade is sliced backward. Acceleration is achieved vice versa.

Physics
As mentioned already, the repeated pry is the counterpart of the sculling stroke. Contrary to other techniques, the generated forces are directly transferred to the boat by the paddle sliding along the gunwale.

Advantages
For the canoeist in the one-man canoe, the repeated pry extends the boat's maneuverability by enabling it to be displaced or turned toward the off-side. The repeated pry permits quicker swinging up into an eddy than the bow sweep. All this holds true to a certain extent for smaller inflated boats too.

Disadvantages
In general, the repeated pry shows the same disadvantages as the draw technique because the direct power transmission increases considerably the capsizing risk in shallow water. Then, use the less effective but more reliable sweep.

Exercises
With regard to the correct handling of the shaft, the instructions given in connection with the draw technique hold true for the repeated pry too.
- Practice the repeated pry slowly at first. Gradually increase the speed.
- Later on, displace the boat in a parallel direction as quickly as possible over large distances. In the canoe, the partner should support the repeated pry by sculling or draw strokes.
- Practice parallel displacement of the canoe when it is moving fast and when it is stationary. The bowman has the better vantage of the river and should, therefore, introduce maneuvers.
- To swing the canoe up into an eddy, for example, the sternman uses a steering stroke or back sweep while the bowman can achieve more pivot by repeated pry. If the boat turns too much, the sternman should counterbalance with draw strokes.

Remember
- Put backward arm around your head.
- Slice blade toward the boat.

Mistakes
- See "Draw Stroke", "Duffek Stroke", and "Sculling."
- The repeated pry is often confused with sculling.
- The boat moves in the wrong direction when you start the stroke. As a result, for example, it is not turned but displaced in a parallel direction.

Paddle bracing
Contrary to other techniques, the repeated pry has no bracing effect. In the event of tipping over toward the paddle, the blade must, therefore, be sliced away from the boat immediately and then used for bracing. For tipping over away from the paddle, insert the blade vertically and parallel to the boat's long axis up to the shaft, with your backward hand at the grip levering across the boat. The paddle blade acts as a keel and has an enormous stabilizing effect.

Swinging up in the C 2. Start the turn with a steering stroke or back sweep in the stern. Repeated pry in the bow. Balance the turn by draw strokes in the stern.

1

2

3

4

▲ Parallel displacement in the C 2. The repeated pry in the bow is supported by sculling in the stern (the draw stroke is more effective).

Swinging up in the C 2. Start the turn by steering stoke or back sweep in the stern. Repeated pry in the bow. Balance the turn by draw strokes in the stern.

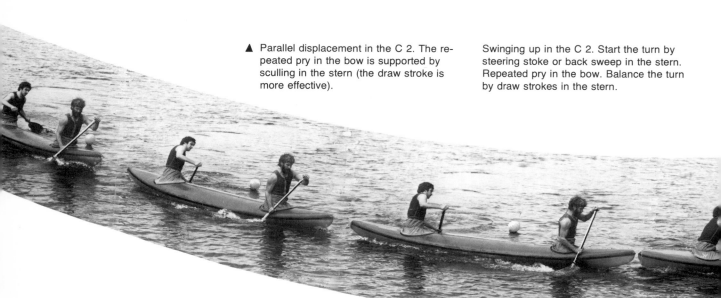

Competition in the C 2. The bowman uses sweeps; the sternman secures with a flat back sweep brace. The boat has been swung up into the upstream gate suspended in the eddy.

Eskimo Roll

Modern wild-water technique centers on the Eskimo roll. On the one hand, it extends substantially the range of navigable waters. On the other, it is the most important exercise in training.

The Eskimos were able to right their overturned boats with this technique on the open sea centuries ago. The Austrian Pawlata was the first European to Eskimo roll his boat. He accomplished this feat in 1927.

Today, almost all participants in competition and many touring paddlers who dare run heavy wild-water have mastered the Eskimo roll. It is always performed in wild-water when swimming is riskier than rolling. The technique as described in the following was first demonstrated by Hans Memminger.

Technique: Basic Form

The Eskimo roll is a very complex procedure. Many factors must be observed and mastered in order to be successful. One basic lesson is appropriate breathing.

- Breathe deeply before you capsize or when you feel that this will probably happen.
- When hanging upside down, turn the shoulders and arms by 90 degrees so that the paddle shaft is parallel to the boat.
- Then lift both hands together with the paddle above the water surface while you bend at the waist. Try to touch the deck with your head.
- In this position, turn the paddle parallel to the water surface.
- With your forward arm stretched, swing the flattened active blade up, out, and away from the bow.
- Simultaneously, throw your torso backward until your head touches the deck. Right the boat from the movement of the hips as well as foot and hip bracing.
- When rolling to the right side, your left foot finds support at the foot brace and vice versa.

Technique: Advanced Form

- Slice the blade out from the water in such a way that its concave side points away from the boat. Do not twist the shaft in the rotating hand.
- Slice the blade outward in an arc as high as possible so that the shaft forms an angle of 45 degrees with the boat's long axis when the blade touches the water.
- When you slice the blade out and away from the bow, turn the blade

1

5

9

2

3

4

6

7

8

10

11

12

1

2

so that is glides backward parallel to the water surface after completing the arc movement.

- For a right-hand roll, the left hand glides to the throat of the left paddle and controls the blade. For a lefthand roll, the right hand glides to the throat of the right paddle.
- The back arm holds the shaft as flat as possible moving it along the hull.

Physics

The successive stages of the Eskimo roll are among the most complicated procedures in sports in general. The process is further complicated by the necessity to hold your breath, the cold temperature of the water, and the difficulty to orient yourself when hanging upside down underwater.

The following detailed information on physics is presented to facilitate your

own practice and to help learn and develop the Eskimo roll. Keep in mind that the roll is expedient only if it works in rough wild-water as well as in the practice pool. In turbulent water, the Eskimo roll can save your boat and possibly your life.

The center of gravity of the capsized paddler is below the water surface. From this position, it must be brought above the water surface. When mov-

5

6

3

4

ing the center of gravity from below to above the water surface, a force acting like a torque is transmitted to the water.

1. The height by which the center of gravity has to be lifted must be kept as low as possible. This requires the kayaker to bend in an exaggerated fashion at the waist toward the side. In addition, at the end of the Eskimo

roll, the paddler keeps low by leaning flat against the forward or backward deck.

2. In wild-water, especially foaming wild-water, the transferable forces at the blade are sometimes small. For this reason, the body's energy (hip motion) is more important than the force dragging the paddle downward. In other words, rolling often requires

The Eskimo roll as seen from behind. Note the extended lever arm brought about by swinging the active blade out from the bow.

7

8

1

2

the boat to be thrown by a rhumba swing of the hips under the body's center of gravity.

3. To increase the torque that can be brought about by the paddle, a lever arm as long as possible is desirable. As a consequence, the paddle should be extended and the forward arm and the torso should be stretched when the boat turns upright.

4. Reduce the moment of inertia around the axis of the Eskimo roll in the crucial final phase by leaning backward even more until your head almost touches the deck following the rhumba swing of the hips. The reduced moment of inertia results in an accelerated turn around the axis of the Eskimo roll (much like the pirouette in ice skating). The reduc-

tion of the moment of inertia should correspond to the general successive stages (blade away from bow backwards or vice versa).

5. The forces which can be transmitted to the paddle are greater the flatter it is held. At the same time, the risk of capsizing again is reduced because of cross-currents which attack the paddle. Nor will one be thrown by

5

6

3

4

the current across a paddle that catches on the bottom.

6. The lever arm is extended by swinging the active blade out from the bow. So as not to lose the paddle, get the paddle across the water and then displace the grip sideways on the shaft with the back hand at the throat of the blade.

7. A "peasants' roll" is one performed with a cross-grip. The same principles apply as with the Eskimo roll.

Advantages

A few seconds after a capsize, you are able to paddle again. Without the Eskimo roll, you must leave the boat and hold onto it, grab the paddle, land the boat, empty it, put it back

The Eskimo roll as seen from the front. The back arm too is lifted above the boat so that the rear blade does not collide with the boat.

7

8

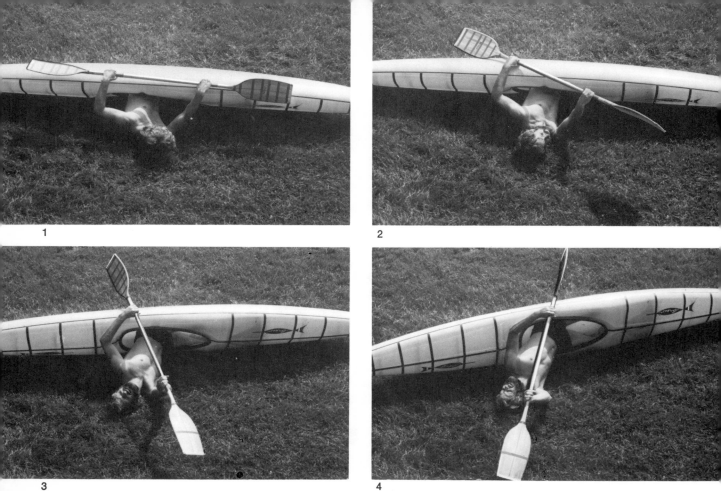

1

2

3

4

5

The "grass roll" as an exercise of the Eskimo roll on shore. It eliminates orientation problems, shortage of breath, and fear of the water. Twist of the shoulders. Concave side of the blade facing away from the boat. Swing the active blade out from the bow. Rhumba swing of the hips. The complete backward lean of the torso.

into the water, climb in, shove off, fasten the sprayskirt, and get under way. In short, the Eskimo roll saves a great deal of time and energy. And on stretches where swimming could be dangerous, the roll can be a safety maneuver.

Disadvantages

There is always the possibility of injury to the head, shoulders, arms, or torso. This can be reduced by wearing a helmet and neoprene tunic and gloves, and by holding the arms in a way that will protect the head. Yet, swimming in wild-water is potentially more dangerous than the Eskimo roll.

Exercises

Begin practice on land and you will learn from the beginning to right the boat instead of lifting yourself. Other advantages with starting on land: you will not fear the water, there are no problems with orientation, and you can take your time without getting out of breath.

- On a soft, grassy area, get into the boat and fall to one side with paddle in hand.
- Turn your shoulders to get the paddle parallel to the boat. Bend at the waist.
- As to the canoe, the author recommends an assistant and a

slight slope. Otherwise, the beam of the boat renders the training ashore unpromising.

- Slice the blade out and away from the bow and turn the blade parallel to the "water surface."
- Perform the same exercises in shallow water about 5 feet deep. Gradually, work your way into deeper water.

With regard to wild-water practice, accustom eyes and nose to the water and be able to orient yourself underwater. Protect the mucous membranes of the nose by a swimmer's nose clip or a skin diver's mask. For practice in water, the following exercises are recommended.

- With the sprayskirt fastened, tip the boat over. The trainer can submerge with you if you are anxious.
- Capsize without being held. Lean forward and backward. Turn the shoulders to the left and right. The trainer helps to right your boat.
- Practice the hip motion with the trainer stabilizing the craft or in a swimming pool. Hold onto a floating platform or to the loop of another boat.
- Turn your shoulders and practice handling the shaft of the paddle with the trainer standing beside

your boat. The trainer can hold onto your wrist while you capsize. In this way, you can practice and observe the sweep of the paddle away from the hull yet still be able to breathe.

- In the same way, practice moving the blade. Remember that you cannot rely on optical control in wild-water.
- Harmonize all of these movements and be able to do them without a companion's help. Then, begin with the complete roll, that is, capsizing to the left and rolling on the right side.

In general, the complete roll is overestimated. When capsizing in wild-water, reliable rolling is much more important than trick riding. The best insurance is being able to roll in both directions.

Remember

- Breathe quickly and open eyes.
- Turn shoulders.
- Put head to the deck.
- Move hands above the water surface.
- Sweep paddle out.
- Slice paddle away from bow above your head.
- Rhumba-swing your hips and lean back (head almost touches the deck).

1   2   3

Eskimo Roll in Wild-Water

- Orient yourself quickly and breathe deeply before submersing.
- Bend head.
- Depending on the situation, you may perform the complete roll immediately. For example, when you capsize while swinging into or out of an eddy, in high waves, small rollers, or easy breakers.
- Delay rolling after capsizing in high roller waves, heavy breakers, at cliff walls, or in front of huge boulders.
- At the second attempt to roll, switch to the extended paddle position after slicing the blade out (your front hand grasps the midshaft; the back hand, the end of the blade).

Practicing the rhumba swing of the hips and backward leaning of the torso.

Pains in the shoulders or broken paddles indicate an insufficient hip motion. The active blade should not be inserted deeper than the throat of the paddle.

Mistakes

- Beginning the roll too early prevents the paddle from sweeping out far enough. This is common with beginners.
- The blade is pulled downward away from the boat.
- The shaft is held vertically and the paddler changes over to a draw stroke. This involves a high capsize risk when swinging into an eddy, for example.

Aids and Additional Equipment

When a boat is difficult to roll, assume the extended paddle position. A highly "nervous" boat, narrow with a round bottom, facilitates the Eskimo roll.

Sitting inside the boat properly (see "Sitting in the Boat") is particularly important.

When you begin to learn the Eskimo roll, do not expect to succeed the first time or the next. A neoprene tunic is indispensable for prolonged sessions in cold water. A helmet or bathing cap also protects the head from the effects of cold water. A flotation bag facilitates repeated efforts at emptying the boat of water.

4

5

Slalom

With a maneuverable boat, slalom gates are tempting. To imitate the experts on television is a goal of many paddlers.

The slalom can be learned only on a course set up on smooth water. It takes several hours to set up a course. On foot, is the easiest way.

However, in deeper water, an open canoe is useful. Otherwise, use an inflated boat or rowboat.

Set up at least 20 gates. In fact, the more gates, the better. Then, several paddlers can train at the same time without being able to memorize the gates too quickly.

Vary the distance between pairs of poles. Some should be narrow, the width of a boat, for example, while others can be 3 yards wide. This trains the perceptive faculty and requires running at different speeds.

The distance from gate to gate should also differ for the same reasons. But it should not be less than 2 lengths of a boat. Otherwise, high speeds are impossible because the course would be too complicated.

Gates should be 4 feet (1.2 m) high. Shorter gates could cause eye injuries to capsizing boaters.

Any lake with a flat floor into which the poles can be rammed is suitable as a practice site. A hard, rocky lake bottom calls for do-it-yourself buoys made of plastic bottles. Enough regulation buoys for 20 or 30 gates would be too expensive to set up. For wild-water paddlers, the use of buoys is reasonable because they do not require an extremely steep handling of the shaft which is uncommon in wild-water practicing. Bricks can anchor the buoys to the lake floor.

The course should run at least 200 yards. Lacking enough gates, you can arrange a circular course. The poles can be color coded: left is red and right is green. Furthermore, a reverse gate can be indicated by the letter "R."

With such a slalom course set up, the trainer can demonstrate techniques and examine the student's boating efficiency and development. A paddler's improvement from run to run can be determined and compared with other student performances. Faults can be learned firsthand. For example, missing a gate, passing it in the wrong direction, or touching a pole are mistakes. The slalom runner has to maneuver the course perfectly while the stop watch records the amount of time required. The slalom course teaches perfect control and precise maneuvering.

Foaming tongues of
currents with smooth
eddies.

Training of wild-water maneuvers

Practicing in Haystacks

Wild-water is characterized by great current differentials (turbulence), heavy waves, and many obstructions opposing the flowing water. Even though the highest waves are mastered by the beginner, the harmless looking eddies frequently make him capsize. However, eddies permit many maneuvers indispensable in running heavy wilderness waters. Each wild-water section is incalculable to a certain extent. Behind each bend, boulder, or roller, fatal stretches may surprise the paddler. Brought about by changes in the water level, landslides, mountain slides, and construction, unexpected obstructions can alter the entire complexion of a river. Therefore, the responsible wild-water paddler goes on only if he can clearly look over the situation and can rate it as navigable.

To learn the maneuvers of starting, crossing, ferry gliding, and landing, practice in a current is necessary, and training in haystacks is especially important. It improves and adjusts techniques for riffled water and leads to advanced maneuvers. To avoid discouraging set backs and disappointments, the following recommendations should be considered:

Training Ground

Do not choose a rapidly running river with slippery steep banks, overhanging bushes and trees, and deep water. Bushes and trees act like fishing nets by catching the paddler and capsizing him. An actual risk to life arises when he is caught below the water surface.

Small haystacks with two distinct eddies downstream can be good training ground. Still better is the junction of a main stream with a tributary, which usually creates three or four eddies. Eddies should be at least 3 yards in diameter to enable you to turn a boat. The tongue of the current should be at least as wide as the boat. On smaller tongues, the boat is almost always in two different current situations, making control very difficult for the beginner.

Smooth water at the end of the haystacks facilitates salvage of the boat. Make sure that a drifting boat can be safely rescued. Inspect the training ground for dangerous poles, rocks, trees, wire, and other potential hazards. Check the velocity of the current by throwing in a piece of wood and timing the speed with which it travels. For the beginner, the maximum should be 3 yards per second.

Equipment
- Maneuverable boat
- Two-bladed paddle
- 2 flotation bags
- 1 big sponge attached to the boat
- Wet suit. In warmer water with few obstructions, jeans will protect the legs adequately.
- Life vest
- Sprayskirt
- Boots in case of difficult portage
- Bathing suit and towel
- Sun tan lotion
- Sunglasses
- First-aid kit
- Tweezers to extract fiberglass slivers.
- Divers' knife
- Repair kit (waterproof adhesive tape is usually adequate)
- Helmet
- Rescue rope

Remove bracelets, watches, necklaces, and rings. If these objects are caught underwater by a bush or limb, they can cause injury or loss of life. Secure glasses. Contact lenses should be able to be worn underwater.

Swimming:

On a wild-water trip, all participants should be good swimmers, able to propel themselves underwater with eyes open. Because swimming in wild-water cannot be avoided, it is important to learn it properly from the beginning. Not only is it fun, but you will gain a better understanding of the river by swimming in it. By becoming familiar with turbulent water, it will not surprise nor scare you in case of a capsize.

Technique

- In shallow water, lie on the back with feet facing downstream with knees bent. This position enables the floater to bounce off boulders without injury.

- Work your way to shore using a back stroke. Pushing off is more effective than swimming.

- In deep water, use the breast stroke.

- When swimming toward the opposite shore, use the eddies and propel yourself across small tongues of current.

- Dive through rollers headfirst with arms outstretched, as you would do in breakers.

- Very violent shallow currents can be mastered by running and jumping.

- When taking a breath, be careful and wait a moment to guard against swallowing water. Breathe as you would underneath the shower.

Physics

A current tries to get every object into a position where it offers the least resistance. A wild-water swimmer, for instance, floating downstream headfirst will be pressed underwater immediately if he touches the river bottom. When back stroking with his feet headed downstream, his body will be lifted by the current if stopped by an obstacle or scraping the river floor. The sprayskirt acts like a braking parachute.

Embarking:

Before launching the boat, check the flotation bags, the adjustment of the foot braces, and the loops.

Technique

- Launch the boat with the bow facing upstream. This makes swinging in or the start into the current less perilous. Put the stern on shore or affix it to a stationary spot to prevent the boat from drifting off while you attach the sprayskirt.

- Embark with the aid of a bridged paddle (see section "Embarking").

- Attach the sprayskirt with the paddle across the cockpit rim.

Mistake

The boat drifts off when you attach the sprayskirt. You lean toward the shore as a reflex antion. There is a danger of capsizing. Let the current turn the boat around completely. Then turn it back into the upstream bow position and start anew.

Mistake

The boat drifts off and you lose the paddle. You can paddle back with your hands. Otherwise, leave the boat as fast as possible and rescue the paddle.

Swinging up:

The current differentials are a major part of the difficulties encountered on a wild-water trip. As a beginner, you will learn this by experience the first time you start into a wild river. Perfect swinging is performed routinely by wild-water experts. You need it not only for starting but also for crossing.

Technique

- Paddle upstream vigorously in the eddy. Lean the boat downstream by foot and hip bracing.

- Swing into the tongue of the current at about a 45-degree angle

and let the bow be turned downstream by the current. Support the
turn by a back sweep, draw
stroke, or Duffek stroke.

● Counterbalance the push of the V
  by leaning and bracing downstream. The stronger the current,
  the more you must lean downriver.

● When the boat is almost aligned
  with the axis of the tongue of the
  current, it is completely turned
  downstream. At this point, the
  strokes used depends on your skill
  and respective situation.

Physics

The tongue of the current and the
eddy have different speeds and travel
in different directions. At the boundary
line between the two, the boat starts
to turn. The currents attack the boat
underneath the center of gravity
bringing about tipping torques. The
tongue of the current thus makes the
boat tip over in the upstream direction. This is intensified by the centrifugal force generated by swinging
the boat up. These torques are reduced if the water can pass under-
rneath the boat, and that can be
achieved by leaning.

Exercises

● Swing up with back sweep bracing
  downstream. Then, using several

Swinging up into
and out an eddy,
roller wave, or
tongue of the
current is a basic
maneuver of
wild-water paddl-
ing. Use back
sweep to swing
up, turn by
sweeps, and em-
ploy the back
sweep brace.

A skilled paddler uses the draw technique to swing up or out. Turn by sweeps. Swing out with Duffek stroke and lean the boat.

sweeps, get the boat back to the same bank as fast as possible.

- When you swing up with a sweep, brace with extremely flattened back sweep.
- Swing up with flattened draw stroke.
- Swing up with steep draw stroke.
- Swing up with Duffek stroke.

Remember

- Speed
- 45-dregree angle
- Lean the boat downstream
- Forward lean

Mistake

A start that is too slow falls short of penetrating the tongue of the current. This causes a violent rotation of the boat around the paddle brace, which becomes ineffective in the eddy or at the boundary line between eddy and tongue of the current.

Correction

A vigorous flat forward stroke on the downstream side stabilizes the trim and speeds up the boat. After re-peated failures, look for an easier training spot. Perhaps you will suc-ceed if you practice only several yards further downstream. You could work your way upstream again.

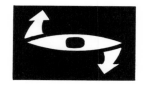

Mistake

The paddler leans the boat poorly. The tongue of the current pushes on the deck and capsizes the boat.

Correction

Upstream bracing by means of a back sweep can prevent capsize. However, it sometimes pushes the boat to the opposite shore. It is preferable to re-lean the boat by foot and hip bracing.

Mistake

Instead of leaning the boat downstream, the paddler bends his torso downstream. This can end in capsize, especially if the boater moves quickly and strongly. (See foot and hip bracing).

Correction

Practice foot and hip bracing. An upstream back sweep brace keeps the boat from capsizing. However, the craft may be driven toward the opposite shore.

Tip

Too many lightweight kayakers, particularly female ones, sit in boats which are too difficult to lean. They try to achieve leaning not by foot and hip bracing but by shifting their weight. To remedy this mistake, convince the female kayaker to master a boat easier to lean. Otherwise, a

2-inch high pad should be affixed to the seat.

Mistake

On swinging up, the weight is shifted in the downstream direction, which usually results in capsize.

Correction

Flat forward paddling can prevent the overturn. In the long run, it is better to practice foot and hip bracing.

Mistake

The boat shoots into another eddy instead of being turned by the current.

Correction

To make the boat turn more quickly downstream, lean forward more and make a vigorous back sweep, Duffek, or draw stroke.

Mistake

After swinging up, you paddle forward too soon – the boat has not yet turned far enough downstream. The current easily presses the paddle under the boat, capsizing it.

Correction

With the back hand, release the shaft or slice the blade immediately away from the boat and use it for bracing. This maneuver is seldom successful. If capsize seems unavoidable, use the swing for a complete roll.

Swinging Out/Landing:

In the exercises discussed so far, the boater brought the boat back to the same shore by the simplest method, that is, by sweeps and swinging up, secured by a very flat back sweep brace. Depending on the type of boat, this causes strong slicing of the stern. With insufficient foot and hip bracing and a wrong back sweep brace a capsize could result.

If you are prepared for this slicing, there is no objection to this type of swinging up. It has the advantage of the paddle always being on the same side.

The following section contains exercises for safe swinging in all variations.

Technique

- With sweeps, drive the boat energetically into the desired eddy. Depending on the situation, several strokes on the same side may be necessary.
- Swing up into the eddy as close as possible behind the obstacle which causes the eddy.
- When swinging up into the turn, lean the boat.
- At the same time, secure – if necessary brace – with your paddle.

Physics

The current differentials turn the boat's stern downstream while the bow enters the eddy. The boat pivots around the bow. At high speed, the turn brought about by the eddy is intensified only when the swinging up is properly started. By paddling straight ahead into the eddy at high speed, the bow is lifted and the pivot point shifts behind the center of gravity. The boat continues its straight course or reacts to the paddle with considerable delay.

Swinging up generates a centrifugal force which impels the paddler's center of gravity outward of the curve. Because the center of gravity is above the water surface, a capsizing risk exists. A slicing stern reduces the radius of the curve and increases the centrifugal force. At the same time, it increases the possibility of an upset. Simultaneously, the turning moment of the center of gravity, which is above the water surface, is increased.

Exercises

- Practice the swing up by means of a sweep and brace at the outside of the turn with extremely flat back sweep brace.
- Then, by means of sweeps and securing at the outside of the turn with normal back sweep brace. Perfect foot and hip bracing is particularly important.
- Begin swinging up with a sweep. Lean toward the inside of the turn with a back sweep brace.
- For very fast eddies, the most effective technique generally is winging up with a sweep followed by a Duffek stroke, leaning the boat only slightly. Sometimes, just the Duffek stroke is all that is needed.
- With great current differentials or in rather flat boats, the stern tends to slice. Then, swinging up with a Duffek stroke, leaning strongly, is expedient.
- When the exercises can be executed smoothly, begin swinging up backward. This will improve your control of the boat and prepare you for this maneuver when the situation demands it.

Practice backward paddling in the downstream direction. Start the turn by back sweeps. Then, swing up and brace with a forward sweep.

Now, swing up backward by a draw stroke or Duffek stroke.

Remember

- Leave the tongue of the current with speed.
- Use a sweep to enter the eddy.
- If necessary, make several sweeps.
- Lean the boat and brace.

When swinging up in a two-person canoe, you will notice a back movement of the boat which is caused by your momentum. This back movement is faster the greater the distance between the boat's two cockpits and the heavier the stern. Deviating from the technique applied in the one-man kayak or canoe, the two-person canoe requires the following maneuvers:

- Approach the eddy as slow as possible.
- Start forward paddling at the moment of swinging up.
- Repeated pry at the bow is better than a sweep.

Swinging up is an indispensable maneuver for wild-water running. It reveals whether the sportsman can cope with boat, paddle, currents, and obstacles. Not learning swinging up is inexcusable and careless, not to mention sometimes fatal.

Mistake

An eddy is not recognized.

Correction

Learn to read currents. Be observant. Throw small pieces of wood into the water to watch the speed and direction of the current.

Mistake

You recognize the eddy too late and approach it too late. The nearly broadsiding boat drifts by the eddy.

Crossing with downstream back sweep brace. Approach at a fast pace. Lean, brace, and re-lean in the opposite eddy. Brace upstream.

Correction

Start ferry gliding immediately. Or turn the boat with the bow against the current and cross to the eddy by forward paddling.

Mistake

Using back sweeps in the tongue of the current, the boat turns broadside, missing the eddy. Each back sweep slows down the craft.

Correction

Turn the bow against the current and cross to the eddy by forward paddling.

Mistake

Back sweeps slow down the boat to the extent that the back sweep brace fails to generate dynamic buoyancy and becomes inefficient when the boat is swung up into the eddy. Due to bad foot and hip bracing, too much weight is suspended on the paddle blade.

Correction

When the back sweep brace becomes ineffective, slice out the blade and pass over to a sweep brace. If necessary, foot and hip bracing must be practiced.

Mistake

The blade for the back sweep brace is inserted steeply instead of flatly and has no buoyancy. Capsize is the usual result under a critical situation because of faulty foot and hip bracing.

Correction

Practice swinging up with a back sweep on easier water. Flatten the blade, preventing the boat from tipping over. Foot and hip bracing should be perfected.

Control

With proper swinging up, the boat is pulled upstream by the eddy. This can be demonstrated by mere swinging up without back sweep or Duffek stroke.

Crossing/Traversing:

Crossing is a maneuver where the paddler travels upstream to reach an eddy or a suitable landing spot.

Technique

- Paddle energetically and quickly at an acute angle from the eddy toward the tongue of the current.
- When the boat enters the tongue, lean the boat heavily downstream and correct the course by a vigorous sweep on the downstream side.

- Brace on the downstream side.
- Re-lean the boat when you enter the opposite eddy.
- Then, brace the boat when swinging up into the opposite eddy.
- On crossing, increase the directional stability of the boat by leaning the torso backwards, putting less weight on the bow.

Physics

The current drifts an object towards lee. According to Newton's "First Law of Movement," the boat continues to move in the starting position. The higher the initial speed, the further the pivot point is shifted backward by the lift of the bow. As a result, the boat is less readily turned by the force of the current.

The more you lean the boat, the greater the resistance at the gunwale, which increases dynamic buoyancy and lifts the boat out of the water.

Crossing with draw strokes. Approach at a fast pace. Lean, brace, and re-lean. Brace upstream.

The boat also travels faster in the current.

By leaning backward, the boater puts less weight on the bow. When entering the tongue of the current, the boat is less likely to be turned downstream while the paddler assumes this position.

By riding the crests of waves, the boater can travel across a river without much paddling. Similar to the way surfboards ride the surf, the boat glides upstream from the crest of a wave to its trough. (See the section "Training in the Roller Wave".)

Exercises

- Cross with downstream back sweep brace.

- Cross with downriver drawstroke brace.

- Cross without bracing. By holding the paddle up out of the water, foot and hip bracing improve, which permits maneuvering without bracing.

- Cross by paddling forward. This is indispensable in competition and on very wide tongues of currents.

- Cross with downstream sweeps. When the boat enters the current at the wrong angle, the craft drifts downstream. This maneuver corrects the angle when crossing.

- Ride waves by steering the boat in a trough so that the craft remains as long as possible in the tongue of the current.

- Cross backward with a sweep brace to improve foot and hip bracing.

Remember

- Speed
- Last sweep at downstream side.
- Lean backward.

Mistake

- You lean the boat too little. The current pushes on the deck of the boat and causes a capsize.

Correction

- An upstream back sweep brace can prevent tipping over.

Mistake

The boat is running too slow. The bow turns downstream.

Correction

Vigorous sweeps on downstream side, perhaps also a back sweep on the upstream side, can correct the course. Usually it is better to break off the maneuver immediately (see section "Swinging Up") by turning the boat 360 degrees and starting again from the eddy.

Mistake

The angle between boat and current is too obtuse. The bow turns downstream.

Correction

See above.

Mistake

When entering the opposite eddy, you forget to lean. The boat begins to capsize toward the eddy.

Correction

An immediate back sweep brace at the outer side in the direction of the upset can keep you from capsizing.

Ferry Gliding:

In the early years of wild-water touring before the draw technique was developed, ferry gliding was the only way to displace the boat laterally. Even today with the maneuverable smooth plastic boats, perfectly suited for the draw technique, there are situations that call for ferry gliding. Ferry gliding can be used to get into a favorable starting position for the run of dams and rapids and for negotiating intricate passages. No one should be ashamed of being a back paddler.

Crossing with paddle held horizontally to train foot and hip bracing. Approach at a fast pace. Brace slightly downstream. Re-lean then release boat to normal trim.

Technique

- The stern points toward the current (contrary to crossing).
- Slow down and turn the boat so that the stern forms an acute angle with the tongue of the current and faces the desired direction.
- Back paddle against the current to displace the boat laterally.

Physics

See the section "Crossing/Traversing".

Advantages

Ferry gliding is simple and reliable. The boater has a good view downstream. The boat is not turned as with crossing which is an advantage when you have a less maneuverable boat.

Disadvantages

On very strong currents, ferry gliding is not suitable for paddling across huge tongues of currents. When difficulties such as rollers and back eddies are ahead, speeding up does not do much good.

Exercises

- Slow down and ferry glide toward one bank and then the other.
- Land the boat by ferry gliding, first in an eddy and then anywhere.
- Turn the boat too far deliberately and correct the course immediately.

Remember

- The stern faces the desired direction at an acute angle.
- Correct course deviations immediately.

Mistake

The boat is turned too far and drifts off course.

Correction

Immediate course correction by a sweep.

Mistake

The boater leans back too heavily.

A boat down at the stern is easily seized and drifted off by the current.

Correction

Back paddle with the torso leaning forward.

Mistake

The concave side of the blade is turned downstream to make the paddle strokes more effective. With the following forward stroke, there is a tendency to dig in the blade and upset the boat.

Broadsiding in Haystacks:

The unstable state of broadsiding in haystacks causes as much grief to the beginner as it gives pleasure to the skilled paddler. Turning broadside happens again and again, usually as part of a planned maneuver. Sometimes it occurs when a maneuver fails and the paddler loses control.

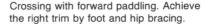

Crossing with forward paddling. Achieve the right trim by foot and hip bracing.

Technique:

- Turn the boat broadside to the current, for example, on the crest of a wave.
- Then, drift downstream.
- Lean slightly downstream.
- Brace on the downstream side. Use the draw stroke as a brace.

Physics

The velocity of a current is highest in the trough and lowest at the crest of a wave (this could be reversed in rollers and breakers). The force of the current is greater than of waves, breakers, or rollers. Therefore, the boat must be leaned downstream to prevent the deck from slicing the current. Breakers or rollers can slow down the boat. If the upstream gunwale sinks underwater, capsize can hardly be prevented.

Exercises

- Drift the boat broadside through high waves.
- Drift the boat broadside through small rollers and breakers.

Mistake

The most frequent mistake is to lean upstream away from the waves the boat is heading into. This reflex action almost always ends in capsize. Upstream bracing, too, entails a capsize risk if the boat is stopped by a breaker, a roller, or a rock.

Remember

- Concentrate weight downstream.
- Lean downstream and draw.

Correction

In deep water, make a complete roll on capsizing.

Training in the Roller Wave

Training in the roller wave, even more so than in haystacks, is important to the wild-water paddler. The roller wave is a typically difficult form of current that is found in heavy wild-water. You can stay as long as you wish in the roller wave (see "Crossing; Exercise: Wave Riding"). The roller wave quickly improves the overall paddle technique of the boater as well as foot and hip bracing. The beginner becomes accustomed to wild-water and to the fact that the boat sometimes disappears in foam.

He learns how to run a roller and how to react if the boat is caught by the roller or if it broadsides.

The skilled paddler in big roller waves purposely overturns and Eskimo rolls with confidence.

Training Ground

The ideal training spot is a roller at the end of a smooth tongue of current. First-rate opportunities can be found in low surf at a sandy beach. But stay close to shore and never practice alone. The roller wave should be 1½ feet high and 13 feet wide. This enables the boat to remain broadside. Rollers athwart the river permit approach from either side, allowing you to practice the left- and right-hand position.

By no means practice in the back eddy behind dams and rapids. Because the tongue of the current drops and a hole is formed between tongue and roller, it is very dangerous. The considerations mentioned for training in haystacks also apply here.

Technique

- Approach roller waves by paddling at a 90-degree angle to the axis.
- Pass high rollers at the lowest spot or where the back eddy is lowest.

Crossing with upstream back sweep brace as an exercise for riding waves. The paddle brace is made with a very flat blade and toward the stern behind the paddler.

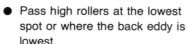

- Prepare for rolling by taking a deep breath.
- When entering the roller, lean forward to keep the boat from emerging from the wave too steeply and possibly gliding backward. At the same time, it is easier to extend the paddle out over the roller and to draw the boat.
- In high roller waves, lean while emerging and insert the paddle as deep as possible into the undercurrent. Then, the boat is pulled out of the wave by the undercurrent. Follow with a flat sweep to right the tipping boat.
- If the boat glides backward into the roller wave, the best thing to do is to capsize immediately toward the paddle blade already in the water. This makes the paddle go deeper into the undercurrent.
- In theory, extremely large rollers can be by-passed in the capsized position, which eliminates the resistance of the torso from the very beginning. In practice, without precise knowledge of the roller, this method is perilous. Risk of injury is high.
- The following technique is usually involuntary and is called the "plum stone effect." Rollers which can be negotiated only by Eskimo rolling

are approached so slowly that the boat glides backward. At this moment, the current presses the stern underwater and catapults the boat across the roller.

Physics

See "Types of Current" and "Broadsiding in Haystacks." The back curling roller catches both paddler and boat. The undercurrent makes it possible to cope with the resistance of the roller wave.

Exercises

- Run the roller by using all techniques.
- Reduce your speed until the boat is caught up in the roller. Then, practice all the techniques again.

Remember

- Fast speed.
- Approach the roller at a 90-degree angle.
- Lean torso forward.
- After a capsize, wait before you roll.
- Abandon the boat when the undercurrent fails to pull the boat out of the wave.

Mistake

The boatman approaches the rollers too slowly. The boat is caught up in the wave.

Correction

If the roller wave is not too high, paddle vigorously and lean forward. Usually, however, the paddler is surprised, the boat broadsides and capsizes within seconds. Then, the best solution is to wait and roll.

Mistake

The roller is approached athwartly and the boat broadsides.

Correction

See "Broadsiding in the Roller Wave." In shallow water, counteract an upset by bracing the paddle on the river bottom on the upstream side. Generally, the surprised paddler capsizes immediately.

Tip

Wild-water paddlers who have just

learned the Eskimo roll tend to perform it immediately after capsizing. In roller waves, turbulence can continue far downstream and another capsize is likely. If the Eskimo roll is necessary again, these boaters could be dangerously short of breath.

Broadsiding:

When you practice broadsiding, enter the roller wave laterally from the eddy. In this way, you can avoid the current sweeping the boat upstream.

Exercises

● Broadside as long as possible by applying the technique described in the section "Broadsiding in Haystacks."

● Be able to maneuver the boat on either side.

● Foot and hip bracing direct the boat. The paddle is only used for securing.

● Familiarize yourself with the roller. Then, move along the wave by paddling and bracing downstream until the current or an eddy draws the boat out of the wave.

● Sometimes you can leave the roller by deep draw strokes near the bow or stern.

● In addition, you can pull out of a roller wave by capsizing, by the draw stroke, or by the Eskimo roll. Postpone rolling until there are no more than a few air bubbles left in the water.

Riding Waves:

Usually riding waves and broadsiding are combined. This can be involuntary for the beginner if he broadsides unexpectedly during wave riding. Or deliberately by skilled paddlers who sometimes put on an acrobatic performances at the same time.

Exercises

● Paddle vigorously from the eddy. Approach the roller wave from below or alongside. (See "Crossing/Traversing").

● Keep the boat in the roller as long as possible by steering the boat with back sweeps.

Running a roller wave. Insert the paddle beyond the roller wave.

- Travel within the roller by putting the boat out of alignment with the current.
- By leaning forward, the boat can penetrate the roller wave, possibly until the boat is in a vertical position or even overturned. In this event, the boat could be damaged. Tightly inflated air bags inside the boat could help prevent extensive damage.
- Turn the boat in a complete circle while riding the roller.

Tip

In the back eddy of low rapids, it is often better to move the boat out by sweeps instead of by draw strokes.

Training in Wild-Water

The first wild-water trip is a great and never to be forgotten event. Especially if the paddler has learned how to handle his costly equipment. Unfortunately, things are often done in reverse. The brand-new boat can be badly damaged on its first trip when in the hands of a novice. The practice of taking untrained beginners along on a trip is dangerous. In case of an emergency, no one can help a paddler who cannot swing up into an eddy to avoid a fallen tree.

A conscientious choice of wild-water for practice is important. The problem is that you cannot choose the ideal stretch of wild-water from the shore. Therefore, the best thing to do is to attend a course or accompany friends who are skilled wild-water boaters.

The river should be classified as easy rather than difficult. Create challenges for yourself by maneuvering. Safety should be the major concern for the beginner.

For basic training, Class I or II is sufficient. For advanced practice, Class II or III. Tackling more difficult rivers depends on your own skill and success in completing the training course.

Tips

Never begin on high water or on rivers with potentially fatal passages.

There should be riskless landing spots. And the trips should not be longer than 12 miles per day. It is better to run shorter distances twice to build confidence. Check equipment before packing into the boat.

There should be no more than five students per trainer. Designate the best student as the leader of a sub-group. Each individual should know the training objective and proper behavior. Otherwise, the participants could paddle away without regard for the group.

Remember

– All participants should stay in sight of each other.
– Maintain some distance between boats to permit safe landings.

Training Objective

The training objective of such wild-water trips is to permit the beginner, who has already run haystacks and rollers, to recognize and evaluate the many technical possibilities of wild-water and to use tactical maneuvers. All techniques should be practiced. And beginners in a two-person boat will learn how to adjust even better to each other. It is expedient to change positions frequently.

Agreement on the course to be taken and prior inspection of difficult stretches are particularly important. A person who has capsized should run the trouble spot again. Otherwise, the negative impression may be too intense.
Besides technique and tactics, the participants must take care of each other. Difficult trips can be ruined by lack of loyalty as well as lack of skill and poor equipment.

Running a roller wave in the C 2. Approach energetically. Insert blade beyond the roller wave. Paddle with strong short strokes.

Equipment

See section "Training in Haystacks." In addition:

- Adhesive tape for temporary repairs.
- 1 spare pair of paddles per group.
- Watertight bag for clothing to be worn after the trip. (Neoprene is very cold at night and early morning.)
- Food for the trip.
- Rescue rope 60 feet long.
- Camera and film in waterproof bag or wide-neck bottle.
- Diver's knife.

Important

Don't forget to safequard the keys to your car.

Exercises

- Before starting, swim in easy wild-water.
- The trainer leads and maneuvers his craft from eddy to eddy. He waits for all paddlers before proceeding to the next eddy. The pace is determined by the weakest participant.
- The student-leader acts in the same way. At this point, beginners recognize the importance of safe landings and leaders realize they must reduce the number of students. It might be wise to divide the group now.
- On easy wild-water where the view downstream is not obstructed, let the trainess, one after the other, lead the group, look for eddies, and swing up. The trainees are responsible for choosing haystacks ideal for practice (see section "Practicing in Haystacks").
- Wild-water tactics are developed from practical examples. All variations described in the chapter "Tactics" should be tried and learned.

Exercises for slowly flowing wild-water (with little foam). Advanced pad-

dlers look for quicker water.

- First test the direction of the strongest current by throwing in a piece of driftwood. Without this test, it is not easy to determine the speed and direction of the current.

- Judge the stretch in terms of difficulty and hazard. Discuss where a trainee may capsize and where to land with a swamped boat.

- Helpers with rescue ropes (see "Rescue Methods") are placed at strategic locations for training purposes.

- The easiest passage is chosen and run.

- At first, drift and try to get along with few steering strokes. In obstructed water, cruise slowly.

- Gradually, look for more difficult passages and run them.

- Paddle upstream from eddy to eddy. Cross and ride waves. Even though this can be wearisome, it is good training and enables the boaters to run haystacks or a boulder stretch several times without portage.

- Upstream paddling with repeated swinging up can be disagreeable at first.

- For practice, collide with a round boulder in deep water. After capsize, drift past the obstacle with the paddle blade inserted deeply in the water at a 90-degree angle to the boat. The current then carries the boat. Eskimo roll after you and the boat are clear of the obstacle.

Remember

- Never fight the power of the current.

- In the event of a crash with an obstacle, lean the boat toward the obstacle (see "Roller Wave," "Swinging up," and "Crossing").

Broadsiding in the roller wave. Approach at a fast pace from the eddy below. Secure with draw stroke brace.

- After capsizing in front of an obstacle, do not roll immediately.
- Adjust breathing to possible overturns.
- Empty the boat of water repeatedly.

Mistakes

- Difficult stretches are not inspected prior to the run. Many boaters are reluctant to land and get out of the craft again.
- A passage that is too difficult is chosen.
- For double kayaks or canoes, the teams of boaters do not agree on the route or on who should steer.
- The sternman reacts too late. The boat broadsides which is usually risky in obstructed water.
- The evading maneuver is started too late, possibly in the wrong direction.
- For fear of a crash, the paddler leans away from the obstacle. The current presses onto the deck and overturns the boat.
- Inexperienced boaters try to evade by back paddling instead of using the sweep.

Tactics

The dictionary defines tactics as clever calculation. Wild-water tactics involve recognizing the situation, finding the best route, and finally applying maneuvers by using suitable techniques. To different boatmen, varying aspects might be of importance: safety for the touring paddler, victory for the competitor, and joy for the wild-water enthusiast. In principle, a wild-water paddler should not regard the wild river as a race-track, unless he is crazy and cannot free himself from the frantic rush of civilized man.

Then, he behaves like a man who gulps down his favorite dish with a stop watch in hand. Such obsessive racing could not stand up against the skill needed for authentic competition. In order to employ tactics, the sportsman should know everything in theory and be able to apply it in practice. First, the boatman should be able to realistically judge an upcoming stretch of wild-water according to difficulty and hazard. The closer the passage comes to the absolute limit of what the boater can master, the more important this process is.

He should be familiar with the appearance, the physics, the effect, the roaring, and the dangers of the different types of currents and obstructions. In addition, the gradient, water volume, shape of the valley, stage of

erosion, season, weather, temperature, drainage area (see "Wild-water Glossary") should be considered. There is also the influence of the equipment, the amount of gear, the stage of training, and the skill of your companions and yourself. Remember that it is less risky to run a difficult passage near a town, when you could jeopardize the equipment, than to do this in a wilderness area.

To be courageous in wild-water, yet not have the slightest idea of technique nor danger, is hardly of any use in the case of emergency. More accidents happen to those who are out for a thrill. Dedicated wild-water paddlers consider kayaking and canoeing as part of their outdoor life and become cautious by experience. These boaters will not run the risk of getting overly tired or beginning a trip with little preparation.

The velocity with which a paddler runs a passage can change the difficulty of that stretch. Generally, velocity means safety where difficult current differentials have to be passed. Correct foot and hip bracing resists nearly all tipping forces attacking the boat. Thus, the shorter the stay in heavy water, the less chance of capsize. The momentum of velocity or kinetic energy increases with the overall weight and speed. Rollers and

other slackening currents can be mastered more easily when the boat is traveling fast. Hence, speed is indispensable for running rollers, cross-rollers, breakers, rapids, souse holes, whirlpools, and all combinations of such currents.

When the stretch ahead is partially blocked from view, reduce velocity until you can locate the correct passage.

The following is a list of possible routes and necessary maneuvers.

Situation 1:

A boulder obstructs the route. It can be passed on both sides.

1. With enough time, turn the boat by a back sweep and continue around the boulder. A back sweep begun too late, however, turns the stern toward the obstacle where it could be damaged or cause capsize. In any case, use back sweeps and accelerate the boat at the right time to prevent any contact.

2. Combine a vigorous sweep, which turns the boat quite far (on a back sweep brace), followed by a back sweep, which makes the stern pass the obstacle. This combination is simple, applicable in shallow water, and has the boat turned toward the obstacle in the event of a crash. Variant 1 and 2 are particularly suited for

shallow water because the paddle is inserted very flatly. With regard to Variant 2, you can achieve a parallel displacement of the boat by a succession of sweeps and back sweeps. In downriver racing, the sweep is varied in such a way that the boat turns on its outer gunwale while you continue normal forward paddling to keep the loss of speed as low as possible.

3. The most modern and rational variant in blocked wild-water is escaping by means of a Duffek stroke. The Duffek stroke will cause parallel displacement of the boat so that very few maneuvers become necessary to evade small obstacles. Because the loss of speed is minimal, this tactic is also suitable for competition.

In the two-person canoe, use the repeated pry and the draw stroke instead of the Duffek stroke.

4. The slowest and therefore most advantageous tactic in very heavy water and through intricate passages is ferry gliding. As long as you can counterbalance the current by back paddling, ferry gliding is suitable for passing any obstruction on either side.

Situation 2:

In a narrow bend, a huge boulder lies in the middle of the tongue of the current. The boulder can be passed on either side. However, this cannot be recognized from the paddler's upstream position. There is a big eddy

on the inside of the bend and a small one on the outside.

1. With low waves, make an energetic approach in the tongue of the current.

Near the inside of the bend, just missing high waves and breakers. Here, keep your boat from being driven into the eddy and turned around. If necessary, back sweep on the opposite side. Turn the boat in plenty of time so that the course curves away from the obstacle. Paddle along the obstruction just missing it.

This tactical variant is the quickest one and is applied in races and clear situations.

2. The boat is swung into the inside eddy from the tongue of the current

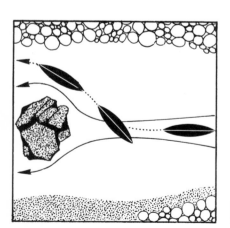

Situation 1.1

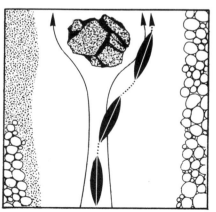

Situation 1.2

Situation 1.3

and turned 360 degrees. On doing this, continue paddling. This variant with eddy turn is preferred in front of a huge obstruction and in unclear situations.

3. By ferry gliding, the boat is maneuvered into the inside eddy. Be sure that the stern is turned far enough and actually enters the desired eddy. This tactic can be applied, like the eddy turn, in front of very huge obstacles with insufficient view.

4. Going at a fast pace, approach the obstruction and pass it by means of a Duffek stroke with parallel displacement. In a two-person canoe, use the repeated pry with the partner simultaneously employing the draw stroke.

This variation requires good knowledge of the passage. One Duffek stroke will do the trick only if the obstacle is not too big. Otherwise, use repeated Duffek strokes, draw strokes, or scull.

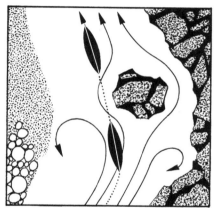

Situation 2.1

5. Far upstream from the obstacle, turn the boat broadside to the current. Drift downstream. With plenty of time, accelerate the boat toward the inside eddy while passing the obstruction. Even though this tactic is not exact-

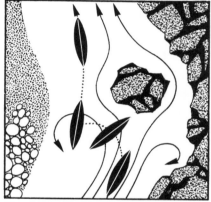

Situation 2.3

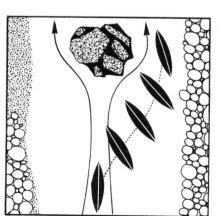

Situation 1.4

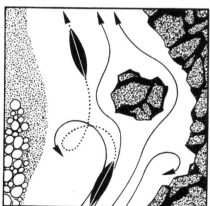

Situation 2.2

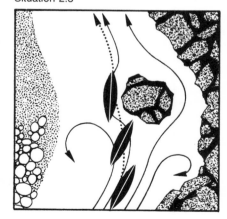

Situation 2.4

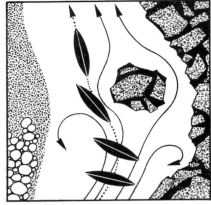

Situation 2.5

ing, it requires reliable broadsiding and well-timed acceleration.

6. Comparable to Tactic 2, swing up into the eddy on the outside of the bend, which is usually narrow. Use the Duffek stroke and normal trim. Within the eddy, turn the boat 360 degrees. In this position, you can often get a good look at the stretch be-. low the obstacle. Paddle out between the obstruction and the bank. If this is impossible, try Tactic 7.

7. Cross from the outside eddy to the inside eddy and go on as described in Example 2.

Tactics 6 and 7 are applied if you approached the obstacle along the outer bend outside the tongue of the current in order to get a better look of the water ahead. At this point, the paddler must recognize that he cannot pass the obstacle in the tongue of the current without an eddy turn. The seven variants described above can, of course, be used in all bends and also in front of cliff walls lying athwart to the river. Trees barring the outside bend can be passed safely by

Tactic 2, that is, by swinging up into the eddy on the inside of the bend, which is the less dangerous side. If you miscalculated or will be upset, the risk of being drifted into the trees or under the cliff wall is reduced.

Situation 3:

In the tongue of the current lies a dangerous huge boulder. In front of it on both sides are eddies. This unclear situation is common on blocked labyrinth-like wild-water.

Apply one of the tactics mentioned under "Situation 2." As to Variant 1, keep in mind that you can pass across lateral eddies without getting out of alignment if you run at high speed and lean back.

Variant 3, ferry gliding, is applicable only if the water velocity is not too high. Difficulties will arise if the lateral eddies are combined with high cross-rollers due to a large volume of water. Take the cross-rollers with a good technique and then swing up into the eddy immediately.

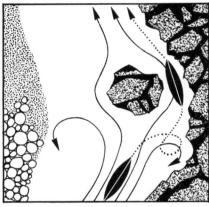

Situation 2.6

Situation 2.7

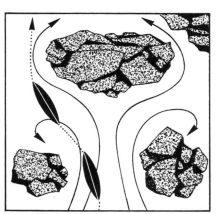

Situation 3 (= 2.1)

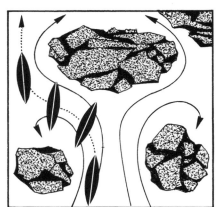

Situation 3 (= 2.3)

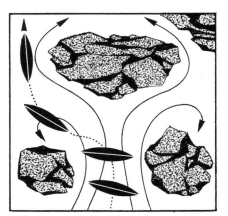

Situation 3 (= 2.5)

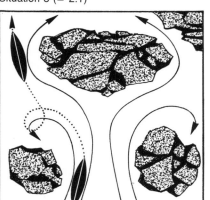

Situation 3 (= 2.2)

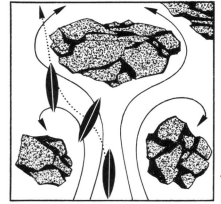

Situation 3 (= 2.4)

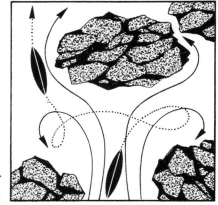

Situation 3 (= 2.7)

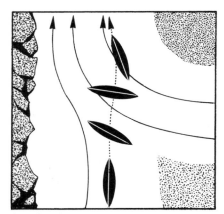

Situation 4

Situation 5

Situation 4:

A very big tributary presses the current close to the shore, which is impassable due to driftwood or perhaps huge masses of water repelled by the bank.

Swing up into the calmer zone between the two rivers and cross the vigorous current of the tributary. If water volume is low, ferry gliding too is suitable.

Situation 5:

A wild river branches out. The best channel must be found. The deepest channel can be recognized by a darker color, coarser gravel, and faster speed. Deep water also runs along the outside of the bend.

You can drift into the tongue of the current, which will often take you to the deepest channel. However, you can never avoid miscalculations completely with such rivers.

This section on tactics is only to give you an idea of what to expect. By mere reading, you connot really learn the tricks anyhow. A book can show only fundamentals. Tactics should be developed from them.

Wild-water paddling is dangerous but it is also free and fun. The "right" tactics cannot guarantee pleasure. But in terms of safety, they are indispensable.

Basic Rules for Wild-Water Paddling

- Never boat alone, even when practicing.
- Never run wild-water unless you are in good physical condition.
- Learn to swim and dive.
- Practice wild-water technique, maneuvers, and tactics before you run a wild river.
- Learn rescue swimming, first aid, and artificial respiration.
- Be sure that your equipment is in good shape before starting a wild-water trip.
- Do not join wild-water paddlers whose skill you don't know.
- Never run a wild river when you don't know its difficult stretches reasonably well. Check information carefully and try to get an idea by comparing it with known rivers. Keep in mind that high water affects the river course greatly and increases difficulty ratings.
- Agree on clear signs with companions to facilitate mutual understanding and nonverbal communication.
- Inspect, from shore, each stretch that cannot be viewed from the

Dangerous collisions
result from traveling
too close together.

boat. Remember that a view from
above may confuse the real difficulties.

● Never run on supposition but only
on sight. Also stretches you knew
from earlier runs might have become much more dangerous in the
interim.

● Shun remnants of bridges, mines,
and buildings in the river.

● During the trip, keep a distance
great enough for safe landings.

● Run every unknown river as if you
were practicing, that is, from eddy
to eddy. In this way, you will
quickly learn it.

● Gauge the speed of running a
river according to the ability of the
most unskilled participant. Grant
him rest stops.

● Be courageous enough to say
"No," instead of jeopardizing
equipment, health, and life.

Wild-Water Racing

No doubt, wild-water sports owe much of their popularity to television. Photogenic, thrilling, and acrobatic, with helmet and Eskimo roll, canoeing and kayaking penetrate via the screen into the little corners of the world.

Racing activities began with the great long distance regattas run annually on the Dunajec in Poland. Still run today, these marathon-type races have spread throughout Europe. The polularity of these races can benefit wild-water sports by making more people aware of the rewards of truly wild rivers.

One of the longest wild-water races is run on the Arkansas River. It covers 22 miles (36 km). Where heavy water has to be mastered, you can imagine the stress for the participants.

Wild-water downriver racing is characterized by running a wild-water stretch of at least 2 miles (3 km) in as short a time as possible. The wild-water must be at least Class III and navigable throughout.

The competitions are held:
- In different classes for men and women, youths and mixed teams, individual and teams runs;
- In the boat categories, K 1, C 1, and C 2;
- As national, international, and world championships (every 2 years).

Boat dimensions are subject to precise regulations as are details of the design. More information can be obtained from the American Canoe Association (4260 East Evans Avenue, Denver, Colorado 80222; 303/758-8257) or the American Wildwater Affiliation (P.O. Box 1584, San Bruno, California 94066).

Wild-Water Slalom

The wild-water slalom originated with wild-water enthusiasts who arranged artificial difficulties in a river section for lack of natural ones. However, over the course of time, the regulations for slalom competition have become restrictive. With the slalom boat weighing 18 pounds (8 kg), and with its strange cruising properties, you can hardly pretend that the slalom competition has much to do with wild-water cruising. Moreover, there are rules which permit and encourage types of maneuvers that are impractical for actual wild-water running. For example, turning in the tongue of the current instead of lateral displacement which has to be taken into account when the slalom course is set up.

Nevertheless, this type of competition is attractive to certain kayakers and you cannot doubt its impressiveness on the public at large.

For the wild-water paddler, slalom boats are much too sensitive due to their low volume and their goosy reactions in heavy wild-water. But the laterally rounded models first developed for slalom competition generated a new maneuverability which nowadays is indispensable with a wild-water craft. In addition, the 13-foot (4 m) boat is lightweight, durable, and fast.

The slalom course should be set up according to certain dimensions. It should have at least 20 gates and be 875 yards (800 m) long. An upstream gate for a left-hand and a right-hand turn must be set up in order not to discriminate against either left-handers or right-handers.

The gates must be adjusted and locked to the current – so-called power gates are not permitted. The current should not move the gates. The gates are numbered to determine the sequence with which they are to be run. The green-white poles are on the right; the red-white ones, on the left side of the gates. The minimum width of a gate must be 4 feet (1.2 m); the maximum, 12 feet (3.5 m). Reverse gates are indicated by the letter "R." International slalom courses can be staged on difficult wild-water or on artificial "wild-water" sluiceways.

Rules:

The gates must be passed without touching body, boat, or paddle.

- The gates must be taken in the correct sequence.
- The gates must be taken in the correct direction.
- The boat must pass the gate keel downward.
- In a team race, the team gate "T" must be passed by all three boats within 15 seconds.

The boat may slice the poles, that is, the boat may pass the hanging poles without touching them. The contestant's body must of course pass the gate according to the rules.

The result of a run is calculated as follows: the seconds consumed in reaching the finish line are added to the penalty points. Races are held in two heats in order of starting, that is, one racer does not run the course twice in a row. The contestant's better time is chosen for the placing.

The penalty points are given as follows:

0 penalty points = faultless passing of a gate.

10 penalty points = touching the pole from inside the gate.

20 penalty points = touching both poles from inside the gate or touching from outside and subsequent correct passing.

50 penalty points =

- touching from outside without subsequent passing. Deliberate pushing aside of a pole in order to pass the gate.
- Exceeding the 15-second limit at the team gate "T."
- Eskimo rolling in the gate.
- Missing a gate. That is, if the boat passes outside without touching the gate and passes or touches the following one in the order of the numbers indicated.
- Repeated approach of the gate if the torso "broke" the imaginary line between the two poles.

In 1972, the Olympic Championship was held for the first time in the world's first specially built wild-water slalom stadium in Augsburg. Even though slalom competition can be arranged in almost any country – it is much more adaptable to the terrain than skiing, for example – it is still not considered an Olympic discipline by the Olympic Committee. This is incomprehensible.

Wild-water Glossary

Asymmetric blade
Obliquely cutoff blade for racing in shallow water.

Athwart
Across the course or current; crosswise.

Back Eddy
The back flowing water downstream of an obstruction or at the bank.

Back Sweep
Reversed sweep used for turning or swinging up.

Balancing reflex
Reflex-like movement in order to maintain the state of equilibrium by shifting the weight instead of by foot and hip bracing.

Blocked
Wild-water being difficult because of a boulderstrewn river bed.

Boiler
A water current upswelling into a convex mound.

Bowman
Person who paddles from the bow or forward position.

Brace
A paddle stroke that provides stability against a capsizing force of a lateral current. Can also be used for turning.

Breakers
An upstream wave breaking into foam from time to time.

Broach
The boat turns sideways in the current.

Buoyancy
Static or dynamic force of the water that lifts an object.

C-1, C-2
Racing one – or two-person canoes in which canoeists use a single paddle.

Canoe
A craft lower in the middle than at the ends along its gunwales or deck. Propelled by a single paddle.

Canyon
Glen.

Cataract
Succession of natural boulder-strewn steps, having a steep grade.

Cavitating
Due to a poor angle to the current, the paddle no longer generates any buoyancy, but rather digs in (see "Slicing").

Cockpit rim
Part of the craft where the sprayskirt is fastened.

Concave slope
Slope at the inside of the bend where eroded material is deposited.

Convex slope
Slope at the outside of a bend.

Dam
Step in the river.

Deep pool
Excavation of the river bed usually in front of obstructions and cliff walls and downstream of rapids, dams, and falls.

Difference in height at water level
Smoothly flowing water downstream of rapids, dams, or raft channels which usually ends up in breakers or roller waves.

Difficulty rating system
Classification of the difficulties encountered in wild-water into six grades from Class I to Class IV.

Directional stability
Tendency of the boat to keep aligned with the current while cruising.

Diver's wet suit
Neoprene suit for protection from cold water.

Double-end shape
Symmetrical plan shape of a craft.

Downriver race
Race on rapidly flowing rivers with many bends.

Downriver racing boat
A craft built especially for downriver racing.

Drawing
Paddling technique which displaces the craft laterally.

Drainage area
Area contributing to the supply of a river.

Drift
Lateral displacement of the boat by wind or current.

Drifting
Rafting. In bygone times, usual method for transporting individuals on mountain rivers.

Drop
Rapid or dam.

Duffek stroke
Technique named for the Czech kayakist Duffek that swings a fast moving boat around and displaces it laterally.

Erosion
The wearing away of the land by the action of water or wind.

Eskimo roll
Technique to righten a capsized boat without leaving it. Invented by the Eskimos.

Ferry gliding
A maneuver to move the boat laterally by paddling backward at an acute angle to the current.

Fishform
Plan shape of a boat with the point of widest beam slightly ahead of the mid-point.

Floodgate
A gate admitting a body of water into hydroelectric power station. (Most dangerous!)

Foaming back eddy
Foaming, back flowing water downstream of dams, falls, and rapids.

Foot and hip bracing
Control of the boat's trim by legs and hips. Counterbalance of the tipping forces generated by the water or obstructions by utilizing the moment of inertia.

Gel coat
Elastic resin used to protect the boat's surface.

GFK
Fiberglass and resin.

Glacier river
River fed mainly by glacier water with highest water level in midsummer.

Glen
Cliff walls rising vertically from the water, "jamming" it in between. Gorge.

Gradient
The degree of slope over 1,000 meters, specified per thousand, or measured in feet per mile.

Gorge
Steeply rising slopes at the left and right side of the river bank.

Haystacks
Large standing waves which accompany deceleration of the current.

High water
Usually muddy with no gravel banks visible. The water reaches the vegetation on the banks. Waves are smooth and long. Driftwood floats in the river.

K-1, K-2
Racing one – or two-person kayaks utilizing double – bladed paddles.

Kayak
Completely covered craft, excluding the cockpit, first found with the Eskimos.

Labyrinth
Highly intricate, blocked wild-water passage.

Laminating
Manual processing of resin and fiberglass into a shell, which is the laminate.

Leaning
To put the boat on the gunwale.

Lining
The process of working a boat upstream or downstream by using two lines fixed to bow and stern, usually from shore.

Longeron
Longitudinal constructional part of the foldboat usually made of ash.

Maneuver
Application of the technique by utilizing the different types of currents.

Meander
A river in Phrygia proverbially noted for its windings. A particularly marked river bend.

Moment of inertia
Force by which a body resists a twisting movement.

Mountain river
River fed from melting snow, springs, lakes, or swamps. Highest water in the spring or early summer and after heavy rains.

Neoprene
Synthetic rubber. Used for diver's wet suits.

Objective danger
Danger resulting from the nature of wild-water.

Paddle brace
Use of the dynamic buoyancy of the paddle to prevent capsizing or to lean (put the boat on the gunwale).

Paddle support
To brace with the paddle on the water surface.

Press water
Water pressed up vertically at the convex slope or similar obstructions.

Quarter deck
Rear deck.

Racing Kayak
One-man, two-man, or four-man racing craft for smooth water.

Racing paddle
One-piece paddle with curved blade and usually a hollow shaft.

Raft channel
A chute at dams through which water passes to allow rafting.

Rapid
Natural or man-made runable obstruction up to about 3 feet high placed across or diagonally in the river.

Repeated pry
Special technique for continuous lateral displacement of the boat.

Return eddy
Back eddy.

Rib
Transverse member of the foldboat frame, usually made of plywood.

Rib shape
Cross-section of a boat.

Rocker
The longitudinal curvature of the bottom of a boat at the center line of the hull.

Roll
Eskimo roll.

Roller wave
Masses of water turning across or diagonally to the river bed with the foaming surface water flowing upstream. Comparable to the breaker.

Rolling
Eskimo rolling. The turn of the blade in the water to pull the boat.

Sculling
Special technique used for the continuous lateral movement of a craft.

Sheering
Tendency of a boat traveling fast to deviate from the course by swinging the stern downstream.

Single paddle
Paddle with a T-grip like that of a spade used to propel a canoe.

Slalom paddle
Paddle with flat blade; an especially short racing paddle.

Slicing
At a defined angle, paddle or deck are dragged downstream by the current.

Souse hole
Cavitation of current differentials in vertical direction, usually foaming, observed at the water surface.

Spooned blade
Blade curved across the palm as well as at the tip.

Sprayskirt
A waterproof fabric designed to close the cockpit space. Worn by the paddler.

Stability
Force by which a boat resists capsizing.

Sternman
Person who paddles from the stern or rear position.

Subjective danger
Danger arising from miscalculations or improper technique.

Suction
Force of the water by which it can draw the boat below the surface.

Swedeform
Plan shape of a craft with the point of widest beam slightly aft of the midpoint.

Sweep
Paddle stroke turning the boat in the forward direction.

Swinging in
Entering the tongue of the current with a boat.

Swinging up
The turn of the boat into an eddy by using the paddle while traveling fast.

Swirls
The current forms funnel-shaped whirlpools which suck objects underwater. Swirls are found between the tongue of the current and the eddy or downstream

of the junction of a tributary with the
main stream.

Tactics
Utilization of the technical possibilities
on running a wild river. Furthermore,
special competition tactics aimed at
beating the other competitors.

Technique
Utilization of the physical possibilities in
paddling.

Terminal stability
Force by which the leaned boat resists
capsizing.

Tongue of the current
The part of the river with maximum water velocity.

Touring paddle
Long paddle, usually unsuitable in
wild-water and shallow water.

Undercutting
Hollowing out of the bank under the water surface. (Very dangerous!)

Underwater floodgate
Floodgate installed below the water surface. (Dangerous!)

Vortex
Whirlpool. Can occur upstream of underwater floodgates. Dangerous.

Waterfall
A drop in the river, perhaps three or
more feet, which can be run depending
on the back eddy.

Whirlpool
Aerated foaming water downstream of
high steps or rocks (see "Souse hole").

Wild river bed
Unregulated river bed in its natural state
often branched out into many channels.

Magazines

Canoe
(American Canoe Association). Complete canoeing and kayaking coverage.

Canoe News
(U.S. Canoe Association). Canoeing
news and adventure.

Down River
(Edited by Eric Evans). Wild-water
sports.

Wild-water Journal
(American Wildwater Affiliation).
Running wild-water.